THE DOUAI MARTYRS

THE DOUAI MARTYRS

GERARD SKINNER

GRACEWING

First published in England in 2023
by
Gracewing
2 Southern Avenue
Leominster
Herefordshire HR6 0QF
United Kingdom
www.gracewing.co.uk

ISBN 978 085244 998 1

Typeset by Gracewing

Cover design by Bernardita Peña Hurtado, incorporating stained glass
windows of St Alexander Briant and Bl Thomas Cottam in the Church
of Our Lady and the English Martyrs, Cambridge. Used with kind
permission of Rt Rev'd Mgr Canon Eugène Harkness, OSB Obl. Photo
courtesy of Very Revd Fr Lawrence Lew, OP.

CONTENTS

1587

1588

1589

1590

1591

1592

1593

Douai College

URING THE REIGN of Queen Elizabeth I, Catholics became known as 'recusants', a term that was coined from the Latin word *recusare*—to refuse, due to their refusal to attend the services of the Established Church. The Act of Uniformity of 1559 imposed as law the obligation to attend these services, a law that was reinforced by subsequent statutes. Recusants could be prosecuted, fined, expelled from London and imprisoned in their own homes. Priests faced more dire censure. In 1585 an act made it treasonable for Jesuits, seminary priests 'and other such like disobedient persons' to be in England. Such a climate demanded that English priests to be trained abroad.

In Flanders fields lies the town of Douai. A part of the Spanish controlled Low Countries and not so far from the English Channel, it was the setting for William Allen's pioneering English College which opened its doors on 29 September 1568. 'Douai College', as the seminary became known, was forced to move to Rheims in March 1578 due to political troubles but, in June 1593, it was able to return and remain in the town of its birth until it was closed in 1792, a victim of the French revolution.

A new home had to be found. At first a large group of students and staff were taken in by St Edmund's, Old Hall

Green, Ware, a school that had been established in Hert-fordshire in 1769. St Edmund's College, Old Hall, was thus formally established on 16 November 1793, new buildings being opened for the seminarians in 1800. In 1975 the seminary was moved to Chelsea, being named Allen Hall.

The northern students from Douai settled only briefly at Old Hall Green before being temporarily transferred to a school at Tudhoe, near Durham, early in 1794. In September of that year they moved to Pontop Hall and then on to Crook Hall, both in Durham. In 1808, the seminarians moved into the new college at Ushaw, the seminary remaining there until its closure in June 2011.

Given the necessarily hidden ministry of the priests it is unsurprising that little is known of not a few of them beyond their time at Douai College and the dates of their trial and death. The spelling of many martyrs' names differ in extant records and occasionally there is uncertainty as to their real name—most had at least one alias that they assumed for security and this might be the only known name. Dates of birth are frequently unknown and, for a few, even the exact date of death cannot be established. Not all of the 159 martyrs recorded in these pages were priests—some studied at Douai but not with ordination in view.

From the beginning of Tractate 84 on the Gospel of St John by St Augustine

DEAR BRETHREN, THE LORD has marked out for us the fullness of love that we ought to have for each other. He tells us: *No one has greater love than the man who lays down his life for his friends.* In these words, the Lord tells us what the perfect love we should have for one another involves. John, the evangelist who recorded them, draws the conclusion in one of his letters: *As Christ laid down his life for us, so we too ought to lay down our lives for our brothers.* We should indeed love one another as he loved us, he who laid down his life for us.

This is surely what we read in the Proverbs of Solomon: *If you sit down to eat at the table of a ruler, observe carefully what is set before you; then stretch out your hand, knowing that you must provide the same kind of meal yourself.* What is this ruler's table if not the one at which we receive the body and blood of him who laid down his life for us? What does it mean to sit at this table if not to approach it with humility? What does it mean to observe carefully what is set before you if not to meditate devoutly on so great a gift? What does it mean to stretch out one's hand, knowing that one must provide the same kind of meal oneself, if not what I have just said: as Christ laid down his life for us, so we in our turn ought to lay down our lives for our brothers? This is what the apostle Paul said: *Christ suffered for us, leaving us an example, that we might follow in his footsteps.*

This is what is meant by providing "the same kind of meal." This is what the blessed martyrs did with such burning love. If we are to give true meaning to our celebration of their memorials, to our approaching the Lord's table in the very banquet at which they were fed, we must, like them, provide "the same kind of meal."

1577

ST CUTHBERT MAYNE

Born at Youlston, Devon, in 1544
Hanged, drawn and quartered at Launceston,
Cornwall, on 30 November 1577
Beatified by Pope Leo XIII on 29 December 1886
Canonized by Pope St Paul VI on 25 October 1970

HE FIRST PRIEST to be martyred, St Cuthbert Mayne was baptized on the feast day of St Cuthbert, 20 March 1544. He was born into a farming family employed by Sir John Chichester and received his early education at Barnstaple grammar school. Only seventeen years old, St Cuthbert was appointed as rector of Huntshaw, Devon, being sent on to St Alban Hall, Oxford (later Merton College), in 1565. Graduating in 1566, he was made chaplain of St John's College, where he received his MA in 1570.

It was at St John's that St Cuthbert met two men, Gregory Martin and St Edmund Campion, who were to change the course of his life by convincing him of the truth of the Catholic Faith. These two men were, when they all first met, Protestants, but soon they proceeded to Douai, keeping in contact with St Cuthbert. When one of their letters fell into the hands of the Protestant Bishop of London, who sent pursuivants to Oxford to round up those whose names appeared in the letter, St Cuthbert was away from the university town, thus evading capture, but definitively deciding not only to become a Catholic but seek ordination as a priest, himself going to Douai in 1573 and being ordained a priest two years later.

After a year's further study, on 24 April 1576, St Cuthbert and St John Payne left Douai for the English mission, St Cuthbert entering the household of the gentleman recusant Francis Tregian of Golden Manor, Probus, Cornwall, acting as his steward and thus having the freedom to move around the extensive family estates and the local area ministering to the Catholic population.

Francis Tregian had been dismissed from the court of Queen Elizabeth due to his unwavering Catholic faith, even refusing the possibility of honours and promotion. This left him a marked man and in early 1577 the queen summoned Sir George Carey, the Knight Marshall, instructing him to proceed against Tregian. Carey sent orders to the sheriff of Cornwall, Richard Grenville, who, with the active support of the Bishop of Exeter, raised a cohort of a hundred armed men and at least eight justices of the peace to surround and force their way into Golden Manor, arresting St Cuthbert and many of the household and collecting evidence of the illicit Catholic rites that were being carried out at the manor. The evidence included a Papal Bull and the wax Agnus Dei that the martyr priest was wearing along with books and other papers.

Having been humiliatingly paraded through the Cornish villages between Golden Manor and Launceston Castle, St Cuthbert was thrown into a filthy cell and clapped in irons for three months until his trial at the Michaelmas assizes when he was brought before Sir Roger Manwood and Sir John Jeffreys. Six charges against St Cuthbert, including the purchase of Agnus Deis, traitorously procuring a Papal Bull from Rome and celebrating Mass were put before the court, the saint being found guilty and the death penalty for traitors pronounced.

The day before his martyrdom, St Cuthbert was offered his life if he would take the Oath of Supremacy. Taking the Bible in his hands he kissed it, made the sign of the Cross and said, 'The queen neither ever was nor is nor ever shall be the head of the Church in England.'

On the day of execution St Cuthbert, having being dragged on a hurdle to the market place in Launceston, was refused permission to address the crowds but the officers present tried to persuade him to implicate Francis Tregian and his brother-in-law, Sir John Arundell. They failed in this, Tregian escaping with his life but being the first Catholic under Elizabeth I to lose all his lands and be sentenced to life imprisonment.

The full horror of the barbarity of the death sentence was meted out to St Cuthbert whose body was cut down from the gallows while he yet lived, falling with such force, his head hitting the scaffold, that one of his eyes was driven out. After disembowelling and quartering his head was displayed on the gate of Launceston Castle and the quarters of his body were sent to Bodmin, Barnstaple, Tregony and Wadebridge. A substantial part of the saint's skull was recovered from Launceston Castle and is now venerated at the Carmelite Convent at Lanherne.

In 1601 Francis Tregian was granted parole and, two years later, left England for the continent, visiting Douai as he journeyed south to Madrid, where the King of Spain, Philip III, granted him a triumphant procession using the royal coach and a generous pension. Tregian died in Lisbon in 1608, being buried in the floor of the Church of St Roque. Seventeen years later his tomb was opened and his body found incorrupt. A year later the English Catholics of Lisbon reinterred him, not in the floor but in the pulpit standing upright: a tribute to the man who had stood up to Elizabeth I, the inscription over his body stating that he died 'with great fame and saintliness'.

1578

BLESSED JOHN NELSON

Born at Skelton, Yorkshire, in 1535
Hanged, drawn and quartered at Tyburn, London,
on 3 February 1578
Beatified by Pope Leo XIII on 29 December 1886

BORN THE SON of Sir John Nelson, Blessed John Nelson left England for Douai when he was almost forty years old, being ordained a priest at Bynche by the Archbishop of Cambrai on 11 June 1576, departing for England with four other newly ordained priests five months later.

Nelson was arrested just over one year later, on 1 December 1577, taken by surprise in his residence as he was reading his breviary. He made no effort to hide his strong faith, answering the queen's high commissioners' question as to who was head of the Church with straight-forward clarity. Thus, he was tried as a traitor and received the set barbarous judicial sentence. Before his execution, Nelson was able to write to the French Jesuits seeking admittance into their order, a request that was quickly granted even though the Jesuit mission in England was not to be established until two years later.

BLESSED THOMAS SHERWOOD

Born in London, circa 1552
Hanged, drawn and quartered at Tyburn, London,
on 7 February 1578
Beatified by Pope Leo XIII on 29 December 1886

ENRY, A WOOLLEN draper, and Elizabeth Sherwood, Blessed Thomas's parents, were staunch Catholics and both endured imprisonment for the Faith. Thomas worked for his father for ten years before preparing to travel to Douai in 1576 to pursue studies for the priesthood.

Accounts differ as to what happened next: one relates that Thomas returned home before ordination seemingly seeking funds to support his studies, another states that he never got as far as Douai. Whichever is true, he often would visit the London house of Lady Tregonwell of Dorsetshire where Mass was secretly being celebrated. That the family house was being used for such clandestine activity was offensive to Lady Tregonwell's Protestant son by her first marriage, George Marten. Seeing Sherwood in Chancery Lane, Marten raised the alarm crying 'Stop the traitor!' causing Sherwood to be apprehended.

Sherwood could easily have escaped the clutches of the law as there was no proof against him but he chose to follow the path of truth when examined about the legitimacy of Queen Elizabeth's ecclesiastical supremacy. Sherwood was taken to the Tower of London whilst, at the orders of the Privy Council, his lodgings were searched and a large quantity of money discovered.

Sherwood was racked twice in the hope that he would disclose where Mass was being celebrated in London. Despite the torture he did not disclose any information and was returned to his cold, dank and rat-infested cell. St Thomas More's son in law, William Roper, was given permission to supply Sherwood with fresh straw to lie upon but not to give funds for food for him.

After Blessed Thomas's trial and execution his family's trials for the Faith did not abate, his mother ultimately dying in prison where she had been sent for persistently practising her Catholic Faith. John Sherwood, Thomas's brother, travelled abroad, becoming a Jesuit.

1581

BLESSED EVERARD HANSE

Born in Northamptonshire, date of birth unknown
Hanged, drawn and quartered at Tyburn, London,
on 31 July 1581
Beatified by Pope Leo XIII on 29 December 1886

AN EARLY MANUSCRIPT claims that Everard Hanse was educated at Cambridge and held a good living as a Protestant minister before succumbing to a serious illness when he began to doubt the veracity of his beliefs. The same manuscript states that he consulted his brother, Fr William Hanse, who had recently returned from Rheims to England as a priest. It is certain that Everard became a Catholic, entered the English College at Rheims and was ordained a priest in March 1581. He had not long returned to his home country when he was arrested whilst visiting Catholic prisoners in the Marshalsea, London.

He made no attempt to hide that he was a priest and was consigned to Newgate gaol. At his trial on 18 July Blessed Everard was examined as to his beliefs on the authority of the pope and the validity of Pope Pius V's excommunication of Queen Elizabeth in 1570. Official records of the trial claimed that Everard had stated that the pope had temporal as well as spiritual authority in England. This was a wilful misinterpretation of what he said. He was then asked if he intended to persuade others to follow his beliefs. He answered that he was unsure what the word 'persuade' meant in this context but boldly affirmed that he 'would have all men to believe the Catholic Faith as I do.' A statute promulgated in the same year of his trial made it treason to become a Catholic oneself or to persuade others to do so. Thus, on 28 July 1581 Hanse was condemned to a traitor's death.

In the days after the trial Hanse wrote to his brother, encouraging him to look after their parents and 'to see them instructed in the way of truth ... my prayers shall not be wanting to aid you by God's grace'. Then, looking forward to his coming execution he declared,

> The comforts at the present instant are unspeakable; the dignity too high for a sinner, but God is merciful ... The day and hour of my birth is at hand, and my master says, 'Take up your cross and follow me.'

After Blessed Everard's death the Spanish ambassador wrote, 'Two nights after his death, there was not a particle of earth on which his blood had been shed, which had not been carried off as a relic.' Indeed, there are more contemporary accounts of this martyrdom than of any other of the Douai martyrs, certainly due to the fact that Blessed Everard's execution was the first after the routing of papal forces at the Siege of Smerwick in November 1580, when a papally-backed invasion of Ireland was suppressed.

Saint Edmund Campion

Born in London in 1540
Hanged, drawn and quartered at Tyburn, London,
on 1 December 1581
Beatified by Pope Leo XIII on 29 December 1886
Canonized by Pope St Paul VI on 25 October 1970

N LIFE, AND after his death, St Edmund was and remains the most renowned of the Douai martyrs. The son of a bookseller, he received his early education in London at the Bluecoat School where, at the age of thirteen, he was chosen to give a speech before Queen Mary I when she came to visit. The young man's impressive oratorical skills only developed during his years at St John's College, Oxford, for there too he was selected to give an oration during the visit of Queen Elizabeth I to the university town in August 1566. Such were his talents and engaging personality that Sir Robert Cecil, Earl of Leicester, called him 'one of the diamonds of England', and he won the notice and patronage of the queen herself.

If he were at peace with the Elizabethan religious settlement, Campion's star would have risen very high in her court. But he had grown up during the reign of the Catholic Queen Mary and, although he took the Oath of Supremacy in 1559 and was ordained a deacon in March 1569, his reading of the Fathers of the Church troubled him and so, in August 1570, he left Oxford for Dublin, knowing that others were now suspecting his orthodoxy and believing that in Dublin he could more comfortably begin to practice as a Catholic. He was invited there by the speaker of the Irish house of commons and, whilst resident in the city, wrote two works: a description of the qualities inherent and to be cultivated in a good student (this manuscript is now lost) and a history of Ireland.

All seems to have been well for St Edmund in Ireland until the repercussions of the publication of Pope St Pius V's bull, excommunicating Queen Elizabeth, *Regnans in Excelsis,* began to be felt. The bull referred to the queen as 'the pretended Queen of England and the servant of crime' and declared:

> We charge and command all and singular the nobles, subjects, peoples and others aforesaid that they do not dare obey her orders, mandates and laws. Those who shall act to the contrary we include in the like sentence of excommunication.

St Edmund was warned that it was no longer safe for him to remain in Dublin and he was smuggled back into England, disguised as the steward of the Earl of Kildare.

He did not remain in England long but he was present in London at the trial and sentencing of Blessed John Storey, making his way to the south coast afterwards, heading for Douai, where he studied and taught rhetoric, being ordained a subdeacon before walking on foot to Rome, perhaps as a penance, in order to become a Jesuit.

In 1573 St Edmund entered the Jesuit novitiate at Brünn (Brno), continuing in Prague where he went on to teach, being ordained a priest in 1578. On 18 April 1580, having been granted an audience with Pope Gregory XIII but still with many misgivings as to the prudence of their mission, St Edmund and his companions, including St Ralph Sherwin, left Rome for England. Reaching Rheims, the party broke up, travelling by separate routes to England in the hope of being less likely to be detected. St Edmund entered his home country disguised as a travelling jewel salesman from Dublin and made his way to London, clandestinely ministering to Catholics in prison and writing publications that were widely disseminated, such as what became known as 'Campion's Brag' in which he described his mission as

> one of free cost to preach the Gospel, to minister the Sacraments, to instruct the simple, to reform sinners, to confute errors; in brief, to cry alarm spiritual against foul vice and proud ignorance, wherewith many of my dear countrymen are abused.

He knew that this was to cost him dearly, declaring 'The expense is reckoned, the enterprise is begun; it is of God; it cannot be withstood.' Another publication, *Rationes Decem—Ten Reasons*—was brazen both in its language and in its mode of distribution. 'Listen Elizabeth, mighty Queen', St Edmund thundered, 'the prophet in speaking to thee is teaching thee thy duty.' Copies of this work were found strewn across the benches of the University Church, Oxford, as the great and good gathered for an academic occasion. 'It is tortures, not academic disputations, that the high-priests are making ready', he declared: he was wrong, it was both.

Through Berkshire, Northamptonshire and Oxfordshire he went, and up through Lancashire, spies in hot pursuit, the saint outwitting them until they captured their prize at Lyford Grange in Berkshire, arresting three other priests and seven laymen along with him.

St Edmund was taken to the Tower of London trussed up on a horse with a sign on his hat that read 'Campion the seditious Jesuit'. After persuasion failed and the discomfort of the cell known as 'Little Ease' (a cell so small that the prisoner could neither stand upright or lie down straight), he was racked and tortured many times over three months, an observer at his execution noting that the saint's finger nails had been pulled out. His body was broken but not his spirit, which he proved to the Anglican

divines who on at least four occasions came to dispute
with him about the Eucharist, the canon and authority of
the scriptures, justification by faith and the nature of the
Church. These were sessions open to the public and
attended by some of the saint's sympathisers who circu-
lated what they heard far and wide, some of the accounts
being rendered as popular ballads. One of those present
in the audience, and inspired by St Edmund, was the Earl
of Arundel, St Philip Howard, the experience contributing
to his conversion.

After a further racking, St Edmund was brought to trial
in Westminster Hall, being charged with thirteen priests,
three absentee priests (William Allen, Nicholas Morton
and Robert Persons) and others with treasonable conspiracy. The charge had been changed from the expected
indictment for attempting to reconcile the queen's subjects to the Catholic Faith to a political accusation of
plotting a rebellion and attempting to involve overseas
powers to overthrow the queen and her government.
Thus, St Edmund and his companions were not tried
under an act against Catholics as such but under an act
against treason of 1351. In order to plead 'not guilty' it was
necessary for the prisoners to raise their hands, St Edmund
being so weak that one of his companions had to assist
him and then spoke in defence of the whole group,
declaring loyalty to the queen as well as adherence to the
Catholic Faith. When the inevitable death sentence was
pronounced, the future martyrs started singing the *Te
Deum* in thanksgiving.

On 1 December 1581 St Edmund, along with Sts Ralph
Sherwin and Alexander Briant, were dragged on hurdles
to Tyburn. At the scaffold his address to the crowd was
constantly interrupted by hostile questions. Standing near
was St Henry Walpole, who was himself to become a Jesuit

and be martyred. It is said that he was splashed by St Edmund's blood, blood that he was later to praise among the verses of his poem 'Why do I use my paper and ink,':

> You thought perhaps when lerned Campion dyes,
> his pen must cease,
> his sugred tong be still,
> but you forgot how lowde his death it cryes,
> how farre beyounde the sound of tongue and quil,
> you did not know how rare and great a good
> it was to write his precious giftes in blood.

Did the government assume that such a death as St Edmund suffered would discourage others from following in his footsteps? Almost certainly, but the authorities were quickly disabused of the notion as the Oxford Regius Professor of Divinity observed to the Earl of Leicester, 'It used to be said, "Dead men bite not"; and yet Campion dead bites with his friends' teeth ... in the place of the single Campion, champions upon champions have swarmed to keep us engaged'.

Saint Ralph Sherwin

Born at Rodsley, Derbyshire, in 1549
Hanged, drawn and quartered at Tyburn, London,
on 1 December 1581
Beatified by Pope Leo XIII on 29 December 1886
Canonized by Pope St Paul VI on 25 October 1970

ALPH SHERWIN'S FAMILY, whilst being Protestant, was not unsympathetic to Catholics. His uncle, John Woodward, was chaplain to the recusant Petre family at Ingatestone in Essex and it was thanks to the Petres' patronage that Sherwin was able to win a place at Exeter College, Oxford, a college well known for its Catholic tendencies. Whilst there Sherwin became a Catholic and was given permission to study abroad, arriving in Douai in 1575 and, after two years of study, was ordained by the Bishop of Cambrai at Cateau-Cambrésis on 23 March 1577.

In the same year as his ordination, Sherwin travelled to Rome, becoming one of the first group of students at the newly created English College, indeed his name is the first in the *Liber ruber*, the College register, with his oath to go to England 'today rather than tomorrow'.

Sherwin's fiery zeal was a challenge for the first rector, the Welshman Morus Clynog, who favoured a more measured and passive approach to the situation in England. Sherwin actively campaigned against this, not always in a charitable way, and ultimately he and those who agreed with him prevailed: the rector was deposed and the college was placed in Jesuit hands with a Jesuit rector, a situation that was to last almost two hundred years, only ending with the suppression of the Jesuits in 1773.

Sherwin set out for England in 1580 accompanied by St Edmund Campion and Richard Persons, a future rector of the English College and ten others. St Charles Borromeo provided the group with hospitality as they passed through Milan. On reaching England, Sherwin was only able to minister for four months, probably in London, before being captured. He was arrested at the home of a friend from his Oxford days and taken to Marshalsea prison. This did not stop him evangelising and being of good humour, calling his shackles his 'little bells'.

From Marshalsea Sherwin was taken to the Tower of London where he endured racking on several occasions amidst other forms of torture, including being laid out in the snow. Sherwin is described as being 'tall of stature and slender—his face lean [with a] beard of flaxen colour, cut short'. According to Challoner Sherwin's 'spare diet, his continual prayer and meditation, his long watching, with frequent and sharp discipline used upon his body; caused great admiration to his keeper, who would always call him a man of God and the best and devoutest priest that ever he saw in his life.' The torture was peppered with attempts to persuade Sherwin to recant his faith, even the offer of a bishopric in the Church of England, but these were to no avail.

After a year of imprisonment, in November 1581, Sherwin was tried along with St Edmund Campion and St Alexander Briant in Westminster Hall, all three being condemned to death for treasonable conspiracy. Hearing the verdict all three cried out, 'Haec est dies quam fecit Dominus, exaltemus et laetemur in ea'—'This is the day that the Lord has made, let us rejoice and be glad in it'.

The day before he wrote to his priestly uncle, John Woodward:

> After many conflicts, mixed with spiritual consola-
> tions and Christian comforts, it hath pleased God,
> of His infinite mercy, to call me out of this vale of
> misery. To Him, therefore, for all His benefits, all
> times and for ever be all praise and glory...

> This very morning, which is the festival of St
> Andrew, I was advertised by superior authority that
> tomorrow I was to end the course of this life. God
> grant that I may do it to the imitation of this noble
> apostle and servant of God, and that with joy I may
> say, rising off the hurdle, 'Salve sancta crux, etc.'

On 1 December the condemned prisoners were dragged on hurdles through the mud to the gallows at Tyburn. Sherwin was the second to die, the executioner's bloodied hands tying the noose around his neck whilst St Ralph

Sherwin prayed, 'Jesu, Jesu, Jesu, be to me a Jesus.' St Ralph Sherwin is the protomartyr of the English College, Rome.

SAINT ALEXANDER BRIANT

Born in Somerset or Dorset in 1556
Hanged, drawn and quartered at Tyburn, London,
on 1 December 1581
Beatified by Pope Leo XIII on 29 December 1886
Canonized by Pope St Paul VI on 25 October 1970

N THEIR ZEAL to ensnare St Edmund Campion and Fr Robert Persons the pursuivants caught other Catholics in their net, including St Alexander Briant, an Oxford man (Hart Hall and Baliol College) who, after having become a Catholic, was admitted to Douai on 11 August 1577, being ordained a priest at Cambrai on 29 March the following year. He returned to England to minister in the West Country but it was at a London booksellers, in March 1581, that he was arrested, even though he was not the quarry for the search party as their warrant was actually for Fr Persons instead.

At first the priest was stripped of any valuables that he was carrying then taken to the Counter prison where he was starved for six days. By the Feast of the Annunciation he had been transferred to the Tower where a letter from the government to the Lieutenant of the Tower, dated 3 May 1581, states the importance of the prisoner:

> Whereas there hath been of late apprehended amongst others a certain secular Priest or Jesuit naming himself Briant about whom there was taken divers books and writings carrying matters of high treason and is (as may by good likelihood be conjec-

tured) able to discover matters of good moment for
H.M.'s service. It is therefore thought necessary that
he be to that purpose substantially examined upon
such interrogatories as may be framed and gathered
of the said books and writing which we send you
herewith. For the doing whereof especial choice is
made of you three and hereby authority is given
unto you to draw the interrogatories and examine
the said Briant accordingly. And if he shall refuse by
persuasion to confess such things as you shall find
him able to reveal unto you, then shall you offer
unto him the torture of the Tower, and in case upon
the sight thereof he shall obstinately refuse to
confess the truth, then shall you put him unto the
torture and by the pain and terror of the same, wring
from him the knowledge of things as shall appertain.

The rack-master, Norton, took the instructions to the
Lieutenant literally, Briant being subjected to torture
crueller than even the standards of the day were accustomed to, including being severely racked on a number of
occasions, Norton boasting that he would make the priest
a foot longer than God created him, and needles were
thrust under his finger nails, all in the attempt to procure
a confession of his part in the fictitious Rome-Rheims plot
and to try to discover the whereabouts of Fr Persons. From
prison he wrote a letter to the Jesuits seeking admission
to their order, a request granted on receipt of the letter.
Tried and condemned along with Sts Edmund Campion,
Ralph Sherwin and companions, he suffered for the Faith
with them at Tyburn on 1 December 1581. Sts Edmund
and Alexander's ministry was to be reported again in the
early autumn of 1585 when their relics were used during
a much talked about, and successful, exorcism at the house
of Lord Vaux in Hackney.

1582

ST JOHN PAYNE

Born at Peterborough, Cambridgeshire, circa 1550
Hanged, drawn and quartered at Chelmsford, Essex,
on 2 April 1582
Beatified by Pope Leo XIII on 29 December 1886
Canonized by Pope St Paul VI on 25 October 1970

PART FROM THE certainty that St John was brought up a Protestant, being received into the Catholic Church before arriving at Douai in 1574, nothing further is known about his earlier years. Ordained a priest by the Archbishop of Cambrai on 7 April 1576, he set out for England later the same month with St Cuthbert Mayne, finding a safe lodging in England at the home of the recusant Petre family at Ingatestone Hall in Essex, the saint presenting himself as a steward of Lady Petre. Arrested and imprisoned the following year he was banished and briefly returned to Douai before swiftly setting out for Essex again, certainly being back at Ingatestone by the middle of 1578.

St John's ministry took him further afield, though, as it was in Warwickshire that he was arrested in 1581, having been betrayed by a notorious apostate, George 'Judas' Elliot. Being taken back to London and imprisoned at the Tower, St John suffered eight months of interrogation and torture before trial, condemnation and martyrdom at Chelmsford. Having prayed at length and spoken to the throng gathered around the gallows, the martyr died uttering 'Jesu, Jesu, Jesu.' So sympathetic to the priest was the crowd that they insisted that he should be allowed to die by hanging, surging forward to pull down on his legs so that his suffering was shortened and demanding that only when dead should the bloody business of carving up his body proceed in fulfilment of the law.

BLESSED THOMAS FORD

Born in Devon, date of birth unknown
Hanged, drawn and quartered at Tyburn, London,
on 28 May 1582
Beatified by Pope Leo XIII on 29 December 1886

THREE MARTYRS SUFFERED together for their faith at Tyburn on 28 May 1582 thanks to trumped up charges of conspiracy against the queen. Thomas Ford was formerly a fellow of Trinity College, Oxford before becoming a Catholic and entering the English College at Douai.

Having been ordained a priest in Brussels on 21 March 1573—being in the first group of Douai men to be ordained—Blessed Thomas returned to England where he worked on the mission for five years. He was arrested, along with St Edmund Campion, whilst serving the Bridgettine nuns and the surrounding area of Lyford Grange, Berkshire. Ford was sent to the Tower where he was tortured before being tried along with Blessed John Shert at Westminster Hall, 'witnesses' who had never seen him before being called and testifying of his conspiracy hatched in Rheims and Rome, places he had never visited, on dates when he was in England.

As he was being taken to execution, Blessed Thomas declared 'I am a Catholic and do die in that religion.' and he professed the queen as his sovereign claiming never to have done anything to cause her offence throughout his life.

BLESSED JOHN SHERT

Born at Shert Hall near Macclesfield, Cheshire, date of birth unknown
Hanged, drawn and quartered at Tyburn, London, on 28 May 1582
Beatified by Pope Leo XIII on 29 December 1886

AVING GRADUATED FROM Brasenose College, Oxford, Shert worked as a schoolmaster in London. On becoming a Catholic he travelled to Douai where he served Dr Thomas Stapleton, one of the founding fathers of the English College there. In January 1576 Shert entered the college and was ordained a sub-deacon in November of the same year before being sent to the English College in Rome, where he was ordained a priest in 1578. From the following year until his arrest on 14 July 1581 he ministered in England. He languished in the Tower until his trial, condemnation and execution.

Being the second of the three martyrs to die at Tyburn on 28 May 1582, Blessed Thomas Shert exclaimed, during the disembowelling of Blessed Thomas Ford, 'O blessed soul, happy art thou; pray for me!' When asked by the sheriff to seek the queen's forgiveness for the acts of treason for which he was being condemned Shert declared that, 'The asking of forgiveness doth imply an offence done, and for me to charge myself, being innocent, would be contrary to my duty ... and I utterly refuse to ask forgiveness for this fact whereof I am condemned, for that I am not guilty; but if in any other private matter I have offended, I ask her and all the world forgiveness.' Shert could have saved himself if he recanted his Catholic faith by declaring Queen Elizabeth as head of the Church in England but he responded, 'I will give to Caesar that which is his, and to God that which belongs to God. She is not, nor can be, nor any other, but the supreme pastor.'

BLESSED ROBERT JOHNSON

Born in Hales, Shropshire, date of birth unknown
Hanged, drawn and quartered at Tyburn, London,
on 28 May 1582
Beatified by Pope Leo XIII on 29 December 1886

AVING SERVED AS a manservant for a well to do family, Robert Johnson prepared for priesthood at the German College, Rome, from 1572, the English College not yet being established in the Eternal City. He then went on to Douai, being ordained in 1576. It would seem that poor health prevented him from returning to England. He was certainly in Rome in early 1580, perhaps having gone there on pilgrimage before finally setting out for England. It was in Rome that he encountered Charles Sledd, an English traveller, a Catholic, who stayed in the city between July 1579 and February 1580, becoming a trusted confidant of the Catholic English community there. He was to betray them all, and ruthlessly too. Nothing about him was honest—he was not a Catholic and even his name might not have been his real one. It was unfortunate that Sledd landed in Rome at the very time that Dr William Allen arrived there too, laying before friends and authorities his proposals for sending priests back to England. It was particularly unfortunate for Blessed Robert that he, William Allen, and others made their way back to England together, for much of the journey Sledd and him travelling apart from the rest of the group. At Milan, they received the hospitality of the Archbishop, St Charles Borromeo.

Sledd carefully recorded all that he heard and the physical appearance of his priest companions, writing of Blessed Robert that he was slim, had an untrimmed flaxen yellow beard, a face marked by many wrinkles and two teeth missing from the right side of his upper jaw. He also noted that he spoke Italian fluently. Sledd later appraised his prey's character: 'he cared not for any in England and they should well understand and also know in England that he would not creep in at a window, for he would go in at the broad door.'

Within weeks of arriving back in England, Blessed Robert was arrested, Sledd's dossier of his Roman sojourn that had been presented to Sir Francis Walsingham undoubtedly hastening his capture. He was sent to the Counter prison and then the Tower where he endured being racked three times and ultimately came to trial with Blessed Thomas Ford and Blessed John Shert in November 1581, accused as they were with the same fabricated charge of a conspiracy against the crown. Like his two brother priests, Blessed Robert had to suffer months more of imprisonment before he and they were taken to Tyburn for execution.

Standing on the scaffold, as the hangman's noose was placed around his neck, Blessed Robert prayed aloud in Latin. When the Sheriff remonstrated with him that he should pray in English he retorted with the words. 'I pray that prayer which Christ taught in a tongue I well understand.' and, with Blessed Robert still so praying, the cart on which he stood was drawn away leaving him hanging.

BLESSED WILLIAM FILBY

Born in Oxfordshire between 1557 and 1560
Hanged, drawn and quartered at Tyburn, London,
on 30 May 1582
Beatified by Pope Leo XIII on 29 December 1886

LESSED WILLIAM WAS a graduate of Lincoln College, Oxford, who then went on to the English College in Rheims in 1579, being ordained a priest in 1581. In the months after his return to England, Blessed William dreamed of his execution, waking the house where he was staying at Henley on Thames with 'a very great cry and noise' as 'he verily thought one to be ripping down his body and taking out his bowels'. It was not to be long before the nightmare became a reality. He was arrested along with St Edmund Campion and Blessed Thomas Ford and held in manacles for six months at the Tower of London. With the Luke Kirby, Laurence Richardson and Thomas Cottam, Blessed William was arraigned along with St Edmund Campion and others for the fictitious Rheims and Rome plot against Queen Elizabeth. Of the four who died on 30 May 1582, all being

members of Oxford or Cambridge universities, Blessed
William was the youngest and first to mount the scaffold.

SAINT LUKE KIRBY

Born in Yorkshire or Durham circa 1549
Hanged, drawn and quartered at Tyburn, London,
on 30 May 1582
Beatified by Pope Leo XIII on 29 December 1886
Canonized by Pope St Paul VI on 25 October 1970

OSSIBLY A MEMBER of Cambridge University, St
Luke Kirby, after becoming a Catholic, entered
Douai College in 1576, being ordained a priest on
21 September 1577. After ordination he briefly returned to
England before once again setting out for the continent for
almost two years of further studies at the English College,
Rome. It was during this time that St Luke had the misfortune to become acquainted with a spy who had inveigled
his way into the college, Anthony Munday, whom he visited
when he became sick. Poor St Luke was also the unfortunate
guide for anther dangerous spy, Charles Sledd, to whom he
gave a tour of the scholars' rooms at the English College.
From yet another spy in Rome at the time we know that St
Luke had brown hair and short beard, slightly crooked teeth
and that he spoke with a slight stammer.

Along with Saints Ralph Sherwin and Edmund
Campion he left Rome in April 1580, setting their sights
on the mission of England. St Luke was almost immediately arrested and imprisoned, suffering from being tortured by use of an instrument known as the 'scavenger's
daughter', a device that worked according to the opposite
principle of the rack: whereas on the latter the human

body was stretched to breaking point, the body held in the 'scavenger's daughter' was compressed. St Luke was to be held for kept imprisoned for six months after his condemnation until his execution.

BLESSED LAURENCE RICHARDSON (OR JOHNSON)

Born in Great Crosby, Lancashire, date of birth unknown
Hanged, drawn and quartered at Tyburn, London, on 30 May 1582
Beatified by Pope Leo XIII on 29 December 1886

FELLOW OF BRASENOSE College, Oxford, Blessed Laurence, after becoming a Catholic, was ordained a priest in March 1577, changing his name to Richardson before returning to England four months later. Having been arrested and imprisoned in 1581 he was offered clemency on the scaffold if he but confessed treason and renounced the authority of the pope. He was polite and steadfast: 'I thank her Majesty for her mercy; but I must not confess an untruth or renounce my faith.'

BLESSED THOMAS COTTAM

Born in Dilworth, Lancashire, in 1549
Hanged, drawn and quartered at Tyburn, London,
on 30 May 1582
Beatified by Pope Leo XIII on 29 December 1886

LSO A GRADUATE of Brasenose College, Blessed Thomas Cottam was the last of four martyrs to die at Tyburn on 30 May 1582. After leaving Oxford, Cottam worked as a grammar school master in London. It was in London that he became a Catholic, soon entering Douai College but, believing himself called to be a Jesuit, he journeyed onwards to Rome where he entered into a novitiate in April 1579. Poor health caused him to abandon his hope of becoming a Jesuit missionary and so Cottam returned to France where he was ordained a priest at Soissons on 28 May 1580.

Before returning to England Blessed Thomas was befriended by the iniquitous spy, Charles Sledd. Sledd seemed to play a most humble role as a trusted courier of letters for Catholics but all the time he was carefully making notes of the information being passed between them along with descriptions of the physical appearance of priests who he thought or knew were set upon returning from the continent to England. Sledd produced a dossier of incalculable value for Sir Francis Walsingham and his associates who were determined to crush Catholic life in England. Sledd furnished the government with a description of Blessed Thomas: 'about 30 yeres of adge—of a meane stature—leane and slender of body. His face full of freckells. His bearde rede and thine & hathe a worte or mole about an inche from his mouthe one his cheke one the right side'

Immediately upon landing at Dover, Thomas Cottam was arrested and put in the charge of Dr Ely, who happened to be a professor at Douai but who had not been recognised by the pursuivants. Ely allowed Cottam to escape but Cottam gave himself up to the authorities when it became clear that Dr Ely was coming under their suspicion. At first imprisoned at Marshalsea and then in the Tower, Blessed Thomas endured both racking and the 'scavenger's daughter' before rendering the ultimate sacrifice of his life.

BLESSED WILLIAM LACEY

Born at Horton near Settle, West Riding of Yorkshire, circa 1531
Hanged, drawn and quartered in York on 22 August 1582
Beatified by Pope Leo XIII on 29 December 1886

MARRIED MAN WHO practised as a lawyer, Blessed William had long been suspected of being a Catholic but this was confirmed for the authorities when they discovered that Dr William Allen had visited his home. Blessed William was immediately dismissed from office and, over the following fourteen years, he and his second wife had to endure the kind of persecution so familiar to many recusants including fines, interrogations and imprisonment. At last, he and his family fled, Blessed William's wife dying in 1579.

On 22 June 1580, at almost fifty years of age, Blessed William was admitted as a student to the English College at Rheims going on to the English College in Rome that very year where, on 13 January 1581 he was granted dispensation from the pope *super bigamia*, for having been married to a widow and, in the college chapel, he was ordained a priest on 5 March.

Returning to England, Blessed William was only given a year's ministry before being captured in the most surprising of circumstances. Along with other priests he had been visiting Catholics held in York Castle gaol one of whom, Fr Thomas Bell, who had been imprisoned and tortured there before his ordination. Fr Bell proposed the extraordinary plan of bribing some of the officers so that he could sing a High Mass there in thanksgiving for being free to minister. This duly took place on Sunday 22 July with Blessed William acting as deacon. As the Mass ended the alarm was raised and although Fr Bell and the priest acting as subdeacon (Blessed William Hart) escaped, Blessed William was caught. He was interrogated by the mayor and then by the Archbishop of York, the latter sentencing him to solitary confinement clapped in irons. Three weeks later, at his trial, the letters confirming his ordination were shown to the judge but, at this point, it was not a capital offence to have been ordained abroad. But it was such an offence to have received a dispensation from the pope, thus Blessed William was convicted and sentenced to death 'for obtaining a bull and popish orders from Gregory XIII pope, contrary to the statute of 13 year of the queen, who had also taken upon him many other indulgences, writings, relics, beads, books, laces and trifles brought from Rome.' According to Challoner, the martyr received his sentence with a peaceful heart saying, 'I am now old and by the course of nature could not expect to live long. This will be no more to me than to pay the common debt a little before the time. I am rejoiced, therefore, at the things which have been said to me.' The sentence was carried out, as customary in York, at the Knavesmire, just outside the city.

BLESSED RICHARD KIRKMAN

Born in Addingham, near Skipton, West Riding of Yorkshire, date of birth unknown
Hanged, drawn and quartered in York on 22 August 1582
Beatified by Pope Leo XIII on 29 December 1886

LESSED RICHARD KIRKMAN and Blessed William Lacey were executed together, both being dragged to the Knavesmire on the same hurdle, giving them the grace of being able to confess and receive absolution from each other as they prepared to meet their Redeemer. Blessed Richard had been ordained on 18 April 1579 having entered the college at Rheims two years earlier. It is thought that Blessed Richard became tutor for the children of the recusant Sir Robert Dymoke, hereditary Champion of England (a role connected to the coronation banquet). This was not to last long as both Sir Robert and his wife were indicted for refusing to attend the services of the Established Church and were forced to leave their home, Sir Robert dying in 1580, possibly in prison.

Blessed Richard began ministering over a wider area in Yorkshire and Northumberland until his chance arrest on 8 August 1582 whilst on the road near Wakefield. He was caught carrying 'mass books, chalice, wafer-cakes, wine and all things ready to say Mass' and he professed to being a priest. At trial three days later he was convicted of 'persuading and withdrawing traitorously her majesty's poor simple subjects from their natural allegiance to H.M. to the obedience of the pope and Romish religion contrary to the last statute made in 17 year of H.M. reign,'. At first he was held in the same cell as Blessed William Lacey but after four days they were separated, Blessed Richard being denied light or food or a bed on which to rest until he was dragged with his brother priest on their hurdle to where they were to enter into the banquet of eternal life.

BLESSED JAMES THOMPSON

Born in York, date of birth unknown
Hanged in York on 28 November 1582
Beatified by Pope Leo XIII on 29 December 1886

DMITTED TO THE English College at Rheims on 19 September 1580 it seemed that Blessed James' desire to become a priest was to be thwarted by poor health. However, at Soissons in May of the following year, a dispensation having been given, he received all the major orders within just twelve days, Blessed James being hardly able to stand for the ceremonies due to his poor health.

Returning to England he was able to work in York for almost a year, using the alias Hudson, until his arrest and trial before the Council of the North. Before his martyrdom he spoke to the crowd, declaring that he was a true subject of the queen in matters temporal and adding, as he mounted the steps, 'I have forgotten one thing. I pray you all to bear witness that I die in the Catholic faith.' His final testimony to that faith came as the noose tightened around his rope, his body swinging from the gallows: at first he raised his hands in prayer to heaven, then, with his right hand, he beat his chest, before making the sign of the cross. He was allowed to die by hanging, the bloodier part of his sentence for high treason not being carried out, his body being buried near the scaffold.

1583

BLESSED WILLIAM HART

Born at Wells, Somerset, in 1558
Hanged, drawn and quartered at York on 15 March 1583
Beatified by Pope Leo XIII on 29 December 1886

A SUCCESSFUL SCHOLAR AT Lincoln College, Oxford, between 1571 and 1574, Blessed William left the university along with the college's rector to join the community at Douai, transferring with the college to Rheims in 1578. At the time of the transfer Blessed William was suffering greatly from kidney stones for which he sought surgery to rid himself of the pain. The surgery was successful and he was sent to the newly established English College in Rome where he was ordained in the college church on 5 February 1581.

Returning to England, Blessed William worked in the area of York with a particular care of prisoners at the castle. It was at the castle that he was nearly apprehended on 22 July 1582 along with the martyr, Blessed William Lacey, after the celebration of a High Mass, Blessed

William Hart sliding down a wall and wading across the moat in order to escape. On Christmas Day of the same year he was arrested at the house of St Margaret Clitherow and taken to York castle. Being tried on 15 March he was condemned to death, the martyr spending the last six days of his life fasting and praying.

BLESSED RICHARD THIRKELD

Born in Coniscliffe, Durham, circa 1548
Hanged, drawn and quartered in York on 29 May 1583
Beatified by Pope Leo XIII on 29 December 1886

LTHOUGH BLESSED RICHARD's date of birth is not precisely known, it can be approximated from the first extant record that we have of him which is of his being a scholar at Queen's College, Oxford, 1564–5. Studies at Rheims culminated in his ordination to the priesthood on 18 April 1579 at a relatively old age for the times. One month later he set out for England, ministering in and around York. It is very likely that he had contact with St Margaret Clitherow during this time.

Blessed Richard's zeal aroused suspicions, particularly when he visited a prisoner by night, thus he was arrested, professing his priesthood, mission, and having reconciled some people to the Catholic Faith. Therefore, he was incarcerated in York's Kidcote prison. Two months later he was tried (wearing his cassock) and condemned to death. Still, he continued to minister from his condemned cell, teaching the Faith and comforting and encouraging others who were also preparing to die. He went cheerfully to his earthly end declaring the words of the psalmist, 'This is the day which the Lord has made: let us be glad and rejoice therein.' Unusually, Blessed Richard's execution was carried out in secret due to the esteem in which the authorities knew that he was held by many in York.

BLESSED JOHN SLADE

Born in Dorset or Hampshire, date of birth unknown
Hanged, drawn and quartered in Winchester on 30
October 1583
Beatified by Pope Pius XI on 15 December 1929

ERY LITTLE IS known about this Winchester martyr except that, having studied at New College, Oxford and then law at Douai, Blessed John became a schoolmaster. His adherence to the Catholic Faith and his opposition to the royal supremacy brought about his arrest, trials and death. Blessed John was tried along with the priest and martyr, Blessed John Bodey but, for an unknown reason, it seems that the sentence from his first trial was deemed unsafe and so the pair were tried again in August 1583, once again being condemned to death.

BLESSED JOHN BODEY

Born in Wells in 1549
Hanged, drawn and quartered in Andover 2 November 1583
Beatified by Pope Pius XI on 15 December 1929

HE SON OF a wealthy merchant, Blessed John was educated at Winchester College and then New College, Oxford, where he became a Fellow, being deprived of his Fellowship by the Bishop of Winchester in June 1576. The following year Blessed John travelled to Douai College where he studied law, returning to England in February 1578 and becoming a schoolmaster in Hampshire.

Two years later Blessed John was arrested and held in iron shackles in the gaol at Winchester until his trial in April 1583 when, along with Blessed John Slade (also educated at New College and Douai), he was sentenced to death for denying the royal supremacy. From his cell, Blessed John wrote,

> We consider that iron for this cause borne on earth shall surmount gold and, precious stones in Heaven. That is our mark, that is our desire. In the mean season we are threatened daily, and do look still when the hurdle shall be brought to the door. I beseech you, for God's sake, that we want not the good prayers of you all for our strength, our joy, and our perseverance unto the end ... From our school of patience the 16th September, 1583.

1584

BLESSED GEORGE HAYDOCK

Born at Cottam Hall, Lancashire, circa 1557
Hanged, drawn and quartered at Tyburn, London,
on 12 February 1584
Beatified by Pope St John Paul II on 22 November 1987

LESSED GEORGE CAME from a staunchly Catholic Lancashire family. Not only did a brother become a priest but, after their mother's death, so did their father—brother and father dying natural deaths. His uncle was the remarkable William Allen, founder of English Colleges at Douai, Rome and Valladolid, the prime mover behind the Douai translation of the Bible and, ultimately, cardinal.

George Haydock began training for the priesthood at Douai in 1574, moving with the college to Rheims in April 1578 and then being sent to the English College in Rome three months later. Having been ordained a deacon in Rome, ill health caused him to return to Rheims where he was ordained a priest with Blessed Robert Nutter on 23 December 1581. The following month he returned to

England only to hear the news, from Lancashire friends, that his father had died and, before he could even celebrate his first Mass in England, he was betrayed and arrested at his lodgings near St Paul's Churchyard, London.

Fifteen months of solitary confinement ensued; loneliness only broken by the visits of Protestant scholars attempting to persuade him to recant his faith. Before the Queen's Bench at Westminster on 5 February 1584 he was one of fourteen priests charged with plotting at Rheims against the queen, even though Blessed George was not there on the date that the fictitious conspiracy was meant to have been hatched. Five of the priests charged were sentenced to death, it is not known why the other nine escaped with their lives, and on the day of their martyrdom, Blessed George was the first of the five priests to die. The plan had been that he should have been subject to exemplary cruelty in order to cower the remaining four priests into renouncing their faith. But the executioner's timing was hopeless, the martyr dying whilst being hung. Those who followed were not so fortunate.

Blessed Thomas Hemerford

Born in Dorset in 1554
Hanged, drawn and quartered at Tyburn, London,
on 12 February 1584
Beatified by Pope Pius XI on 15 December 1929

escribed as 'a short man with a dark beard, severe of look but of a sweet disposition', Blessed Thomas was educated at Hart Hall and St John's College, Oxford, graduating in 1575. Subsequently becoming a Catholic, he was admitted to the English College at

Rheims in July 1580 but was almost immediately dispatched to the English College in Rome where he was ordained a priest in March 1583 by Bishop Goldwell of St Asaph, the last bishop from the reign of Queen Mary I.

Returning homewards in April he stopped at Rheims, arriving in England in June. By the end of the year he had been caught and imprisoned in the Marshalsea before trial, condemnation and execution with his brother priests.

BLESSED JAMES FENN

Born in Montacute, Somerset, circa 1540
Hanged, drawn and quartered at Tyburn, London,
on 12 February 1584
Beatified by Pope Pius XI on 15 December 1929

NE OF THREE brothers who became priests, Blessed James was the only one to be martyred. He had been a chorister at New College, Oxford, before being admitted to Corpus Christi in 1554. In 1560 he was expelled from his college for refusing to take the Oath of Supremacy, going on to work as a tutor at Gloucester Hall and a schoolmaster in Somerset. Priesthood was not his first vocation for he was married with two children, Frances and John, but after his wife died, he travelled to Rheims and entered the English College in 1579 being ordained at Châlons the following year after which he returned to England.

He seems to have been successfully hunted down very quickly, being arrested at Brimpton, Somerset, and imprisoned at Ilchester before being taken to the Marshalsea, London, where over two years he ministered as a priest to fellow prisoners. After almost two years in prison he was brought to stand trial with George Haydock, accused of plotting in Rome with him to kill the queen. Neither of the priests had ever met before and Blessed James had never been to Rome. For this fiction he was condemned, being offered his freedom while in prison after the trial if he would make the Oath of Supremacy, which he refused to do, his daughter, Frances, witnessing his death and receiving his blessing before being martyred.

BLESSED JOHN NUTTER

Born in Clitheroe, Lancashire, date of birth unknown
Hanged, drawn and quartered at Tyburn, London,
on 12 February 1584
Beatified by Pope Pius XI on 15 December 1929

HE FOURTH OF the priests to die at Tyburn on 12 February 1584, Blessed John and his brother, the martyr Blessed Robert Nutter, commenced their studies for the priesthood together on 23 August 1579, Blessed John having previously studied at St John's College, Cambridge. He was ordained a priest in September 1582, leaving for England two months later.

By the time that he set foot on shore at Dunwich, Suffolk, he was suffering from a high fever that was to prevent him from travelling on. Arrested on 15 January 1583, an attempt to claim that he was a merchant from York collapsed with the discovery of five hundred catechisms and fifteen copies of the newly published Douai-Rheims New Testament in his luggage. Sent first to the Marshalsea, after he had been tried and sentenced Blessed John was thrown into the notorious Pit at the Tower of London where he found his brother, Robert, who had been arrested in Oxford just five days before, and where he awaited his death.

Blessed John Munden

Born in Mapperton, Dorset, in 1543
Hanged, drawn and quartered at Tyburn, London,
on 12 February 1584
Beatified by Pope Pius XI on 15 December 1929

INCHESTER COLLEGE AND New College, Oxford, where he became a Fellow in 1562, were the establishments that educated Blessed John. In 1566 he was expelled from his college, almost certainly on account of his religious convictions, going on to make a living as a schoolmaster in Dorset.

In 1580 he became a member of the college at Rheims, where he received minor orders, before being sent to the English College, Rome, in July 1582, where he was ordained a priest. On 6 August 1582 he set out for the English mission and was arrested as he stepped ashore at Dover. A bribe of £15 secured his escape but he was caught again in February 1583 on Hounslow Heath travelling from Winchester to London. Committed to the Tower, he was interrogated by Sir Francis Walsingham who accused him of plotting to kill the queen. The truth, that this was not so, would never save the priest's life. He was found guilty at trial but looked so joyful after sentence was pronounced that some thought that he had been acquitted. On the day of his martyrdom Blessed John was the last to die, having witnessed his four priestly companions butchered before he was executed. The night before his death he wrote to his cousin, Blessed Edmund

Duke, saying 'I am now warned to prepare against tomorrow to go to die, and yet I hope in Jesus Christ to live for ever ... '

1585

Blessed Thomas Alfield

Born in Gloucester in 1552
Hanged at Tyburn, London, on 6 July 1585
Beatified by Pope Pius XI on 15 December 1929

BORN THE SON of a master at Gloucester School, Blessed Thomas was educated at Eton and King's College, Cambridge, following in his father's footsteps by becoming a Fellow at King's. A year after becoming a Catholic in 1575, and thus renouncing his Fellowship, he visited the English College at Douai for a few months from September 1576, returning to the college, by then in Rheims, in September 1580 to commence studies. The following year, on 4 March, he was ordained a priest at Châlons and returned to England at the end of the month, using the alias Badger. He reconciled Blessed William Dean to the Catholic Faith and witnessed the execution of St Edmund Campion and his companions at Tyburn on 1 December 1581. Only five months later, on 7 April 1582, he was arrested himself, perhaps betrayed by his own father.

According to some accounts, torture in the Tower broke the martyr who renounced his faith and was released from prison in September 1582, other accounts make no mention of such apostasy. However it came about, it is certain that in 1583 Blessed Thomas was once again in Gloucester having, according to a letter of William Allen, visited Douai. During this period Blessed Thomas wrote an account of the martyrdom of St Edmund Campion and his companions.

Blessed Thomas then seems to have moved to London for it was with a dyer, the Venerable Thomas Webley, that he imported and distributed in the parish of All Saints, Bread Street, five to six hundred copies of William Allen's book, *Modest Defence of the English Catholiques*, a tract written by Allen that argued that Catholics were being persecuted for treason, not for their religion. In June 1585 the two were arrested and relentlessly tortured in the hope that they might reveal the names of those who had received the books. Having been held in Newgate prison, on 5 July they were charged with distributing the tracts, a crime punishable by death as the books were held to be written against the queen. The judge—a fellow old Etonian—held that Blessed Thomas was 'bold, stout and arrogant' and condemned him, along with the Venerable Thomas Webley, to death. A reprieve for Blessed Thomas Alfield arrived too late to save him—it is unknown why such a reprieve was granted. As the two martyrs were convicted as felons, not traitors, they were hanged but not drawn and quartered. Fr Robert Persons was to comment on the sentencing that 'It is thus that these men answer our books—by hanging us'. A brother of Blessed Thomas Alfield, Robert, who had also become a Catholic became a servant of Fr Persons, but he later renounced the Faith and 'did great harm', according to Fr Persons, probably as an informer.

Blessed Hugh Taylor

Born in Durham circa 1560
Hanged, drawn and quartered at York on 26 November 1585
Beatified by Pope St John Paul II on 22 November 1987

BLESSED HUGH WAS ordained a priest on 13 June 1584 after having spent two years at the English College in Rheims. By March 1585 he had returned to England and was ministering in Yorkshire and Durham: within eight months he was tried and martyred. He was not tried alone but with a layman, Blessed Marmaduke Bowes, who had offered him hospitality and, inquiring after the priest once he had been arrested, found himself also arrested for assisting the priest and ultimately martyred the day after him.

In the year after the martyrdoms, an anonymous author wrote,

> Taylor, having been condemned to death in company with a layman on Thursday, was also to celebrate Mass and recite his Office on the Friday. Then he said, 'How happy I should be if on this day on which Christ died for me, I might encounter death for him.' Scarcely had he said this, when the officer unexpectedly came to lead him off to execution, and leaving the layman for Saturday, (the customary day for executions) put him immediately to death.

1586

BLESSED EDWARD STRANSHAM

Born in Oxford circa 1557
Hanged, drawn and quartered at Tyburn, London,
on 21 January 1586
Beatified by Pope Pius XI on 15 December 1929

LESSED EDWARD GRADUATED from St John's College, Oxford, circa 1576, became a Catholic and was admitted to Douai College in 1577, transferring with the college to Rheims the following year but returning to England due to poor health within months. In 1579 he returned to the college, this time persevering until his priestly ordination at Soissons in December 1580 but not setting out for England until 30 June 1580, travelling along with Blessed Nicholas Woodfen.

Nothing is known of his ministry except that he brought ten converts from Oxford to Douai College in 1583, remaining there for five months before travelling to Paris where he stayed for a further year and a half, becoming gravely ill. On 17 July 1585 he was arrested whilst saying Mass at a house on Bishopsgate Street

Without in London and, after trial, martyred along with
Blessed Nicholas Woodfen.

Blessed Nicholas Woodfen

Born at Leominster, Herefordshire, circa 1550
Hanged, drawn and quartered at Tyburn, London, on 21
January 1586
Beatified by Pope St John Paul II on 22 November 1987

The writings of a schoolfriend, Fr Richard Davies, state
that Blessed Nicholas' surname was originally 'Wheeler'
and that he was 'held for one of the best scholars in the
school'. This remark is borne out by the fact that he
assisted St Swithun Wells at his Wiltshire school. Blessed
Nicholas entered the English College at Rheims on 27
December 1579 and was ordained a priest by the Bishop
of Châlons-sur-Marne on the feast of the Annunciation
1581, departing for England on 30 June in the same year.

At first Blessed Nicholas ministered in London but,
according to Fr Davies, he 'declared unto me, (the tears
standing in his eyes) that he had neither money to buy him
meat nor scarce any clothes upon his back. I pitied his case,
comforted him and gave him such money as I had then
present.'. With Fr Davies' help, he was able to secure a
lodging in Fleet Street, dressing in the kind of gown that
the lawyers working at the nearby Inns of Court would
wear, thus being able to mingle and minister among them
quite freely, earning for himself the particular hatred of
Thomas Dodwell, a government spy, who reported that
the priest was one of 'the most traitorous papists of that
seminary of Satan' and that he needed to be caught
quickly. Becoming aware of impending danger, Blessed

Nicholas left Fleet Street for Fr Davies' lodgings in Hoxton where they both narrowly escaped capture during an ensuing raid by hiding in a secret priests' hole. It is not known when the martyr was caught but his trial was held on 19 January 1586 before he suffered with Blessed Edward Stransham at Tyburn.

BLESSED RICHARD SERGEANT

Born in Gloucester circa 1550
Hanged, drawn and quartered at Tyburn, London,
on 20 April 1586
Beatified by Pope St John Paul II on 22 November 1987

PART FROM THE fact that Blessed Richard graduated from Oxford University in February 1571, virtually nothing is known of his life before he entered the English College at Rheims on 25 July 1581, being ordained a priest at Laon on 7 April 1583 and departing for the English mission five months later on 10 September. After these recorded facts, little else is known for certain of Blessed Richard's ministry. He is thought to have worked in the London area and later chroniclers referred to 'his fruitful labours' and to his learning. Along with Blessed William Thomson, Blessed John was tried at the Old Bailey on 18 April 1586, both being executed together for being priests two days later.

Blessed William Thomson

Born at Blackburn, Lancashire, circa 1560
Hanged, drawn and quartered at Tyburn, London,
on 20 April 1586
Beatified by Pope St John Paul II on 22 November
1987

LESSED WILLIAM ENTERED the English College at Rheims on 28 May 1583, being ordained a priest on 31 March the following year. Thanks to the reports of government spies, it is known that Blessed William was working in London in 1585.

There are two accounts of Blessed William's arrest, both suggest that this happened after Mass, one account saying the Mass was at Bishopsgate Without and attended by the brother and husband of Saint Anne Line (who were also arrested), the other account stating that the Mass was at a house at Harrow on the Hill. This discrepancy notwithstanding, it is certain that he and Blessed Richard Sergeant appeared together before the Newgate Sessions at the Old Bailey on 18 April 1586, both dying together at Tyburn.

Blessed Robert Anderton

Born on the Isle of Man in 1560

Blessed William Marsden

Born in Goosnargh, Lancashire, circa 1560

*Both hanged, drawn and quartered at Newport, Isle
of Wight, on 25 April 1586
Beatified by Pope Pius XI on 15 December 1929*

OTH MARTYRS WERE friends, both being educated at a grammar school in Rivington, Lancashire, before proceeding to Oxford, Blessed
Robert to Brasenose College and Blessed William at St
Mary's Hall, and both went to Douai College at Rheims
together to be received into the Church and, in 1580,
entering the college, the former being ordained in 1584,
the latter in 1585. Together they left the college in February 1586 being almost immediately apprehended on the
Isle of Wight after their ship was forced to take refuge
there during a storm. At their trial in Winchester, strongly
protesting their loyalty to the queen and arguing that there
was no proof that they had intended to set foot in England
but were forced ashore by the storm, they requested that
they be sent to be examined by the Privy Council. They
were sent to London, the Council finding them guilty as
the court at Winchester had found them and sent them
back to Winchester. The Council also ordered that a royal
proclamation outlining their arrest, trial and examination
should be exhibited and read out by the sheriff, the only
instance of such a proclamation ordering the death of
priests, the execution happening on the Isle of Wight near
the place where they had landed.

BLESSED FRANCIS INGLEBY

Born at Ripley Castle, West Yorkshire, circa 1550
Hanged, drawn and quartered at York on 3 June
1586
Beatified by Pope St John Paul II on 22 November
1987

HE FOURTH SON of Sir William Ingleby and his wife, Anne, Blessed Francis was educated at Brasenose College, Oxford, before proceeding to study law at the Inner Temple in London. He arrived in Rheims on 8 August 1582 being ordained a priest the following year on 17 December. Between 1584 and his arrest in 1586 Blessed Francis ministered in and around the city of York, being one of the priests that St Margaret Clitherow was accused of harbouring. When she was arrested on 10 March 1586, Blessed Francis made his way out of the city to safety but when a man who was accompanying him took his leave of the priest, showing what seemed to those who noticed too much respect to a labourer, their curiosity was aroused and Blessed Francis was arrested, appearing before the Council of the North on 2 June. On hearing his sentence, he is said to have exclaimed, "*Credo videre bona Domini in terra viventium*" (*I believe to see the good things of our Lord: in the land of the living*) and, as he was taken back to prison after the trial the Catholics of York transformed what was meant to have been a humiliating journey into a triumphant celebration with cheering men and women leaning out of their windows, asking for the priest's blessing.

Blessed John Fingley

Born in Barmby-in-the-Marsh, East Riding of York-
shire, in 1553
Hanged, drawn and quartered at York on 8 August
1586
Beatified by Pope St John Paul II on 22 November
1987

GIFTED MAN FROM a poor family, Blessed John secured a place at Gonville and Caius College, Cambridge, by paying his way as a college servant there. The new College Master, Dr Thomas Legge (chosen by the college's founder, John Caius, as his successor as Master) appointed Fingley to the important role of Butler. Legge clearly believed in religious toleration—at least six of the college's students became Jesuits, one a Benedictine and ten became Catholic priests. The Fellows, however, were less tolerant and complained about the appointment of Fingley who was described as 'an arrant papist', even a priest in disguise who had said Mass in 'the Master's greater chamber over the parlour'.

Not a priest yet, Blessed John left Cambridge without a degree and was admitted to the English College at Rheims on 13 February 1580, being ordained a priest on the Feast of the Annunciation the next year before returning to minister in England for the next four years.

Blessed John was arrested in Yorkshire in June 1585 and incarcerated in a dark dungeon at Peter Prison, York. Above the cell was being a held a stubborn recusant, Frances Webster, who managed to lift a grate in the floor of her cell, letting a little light into the darkness below and encouraging the priest to remain strong. Blessed John was condemned to death for his priesthood and for reconciling subjects of the queen to the Catholic Faith. The martyr's mother is thought to have been present at his execution.

Blessed John Sandys

Born in Lancashire about 1550–55
Hanged, drawn and quartered at Gloucester on 11 August 1586
Beatified by Pope St John Paul II on 22 November 1987

Having graduated in 1573, Blessed John left Oriel College, Oxford, to become tutor to the children of Admiral Sir William Winter at Lydney, Gloucestershire. Upon becoming a Catholic, Blessed John travelled to Rheims and entered the English College there on 4 June 1583, being ordained a priest at the city's cathedral on 31 March the following year.

Seven months later Blessed John, along with two other priests, returned to England, sailing from Dieppe to Rye, then continuing alone to Gloucestershire where he would be able to rely on friends for help. For two years he ministered in the area until he was caught up in a revenge attack on the Anglican Dean of Lydney. It is uncertain if Blessed John was staying with the dean or only visiting him but the Dean's enemies found out that his visitor was a priest and informed the authorities, principally aiming to damage the dean. Blessed John was arrested but the dean was not as he insisted that he had no idea that the man he was entertaining was a priest. Those who used Blessed John as a trap to ruin the dean visited the priest in prison to apologize but this was not going to stop the law taking its course.

By all accounts Blessed John's martyrdom was immensely cruel. A practiced executioner could not be had, so 'At last they found a most base companion, who was yet ashamed to be seen in that bloody action, for he blacked and disfigured his face, and got an old rusty knife full of teeth like a sickle, with which he killed him', disgusting even those accustomed to such barbarous deeds.

BLESSED JOHN LOWE

Born in London in 1553
Hanged, drawn and quartered at Tyburn, London,
on 8 October 1586
Beatified by Pope St John Paul II on 22 November
1987

NAMED AFTER HIS father, Blessed John was admitted to Douai circa 1575 but was sent on to the English College, Rome, in 1581 being ordained a priest in September of the following year. Having mulled over the idea of seeking admittance into the Society of Jesus, he returned to London as a secular priest in late December 1583. Government spies were aware of him but it was not until 11 May 1584 that he was arrested and committed to the Clink prison where he was tricked into taking the cunning apostate priest and informer Antony Tyrol into his confidence, providing the state with the information that they needed to ensure his execution. Blessed John was tried along with Blessed John Adams and Blessed Robert Dibdale, with whom he was also martyred.

Blessed John Adams

Born at Winterbourne St Martin, Dorsetshire, circa 1543
Hanged, drawn and quartered at Tyburn, London, on 8 October 1586
Beatified by Pope St John Paul II on 22 November 1987

inistry in the Church of England preceded conversion and a year's study at the English College in Rheims before his ordination as a priest at Soissons on 17 December 1580. He set out for England at the end of March 1581 but, on landing at Rye, he was immediately apprehended and sent to London as a prisoner. He escaped and returned to Rheims setting out for the English mission again in June 1583 and arrived in the country unnoticed and being described at this time as

> about forty years of age, of average height, with a dark beard, a sprightly look and black eyes. He was a very good controversialist, straightforward, very pious, and pre-eminently a man of hard work. He laboured very strenuously at Winchester and in Hampshire, where he helped many, especially of the poorer classes.

He was arrested again on 7 March 1584 and, after spending eighteen months in the Marshalsea prison, he was banished, returning to Rheims only to promptly turn round and head back for Winchester, where he was arrested for the final time on 19 December 1585 and incarcerated in the Clink prison in London. Like Blessed John Lowe, he was duped by Antony Tyrrell, the gathered evidence ensuring his death sentence.

BLESSED ROBERT DIBDALE

Born at Shottery, Warwickshire, circa 1558
Hanged, drawn and quartered at Tyburn, London,
on 8 October 1586
Beatified by Pope St John Paul II on 22 November
1987

HE VILLAGE OF SHOTTERY, the birthplace of William Shakespeare's wife, lay in the parish of Stratford-upon-Avon and it is possible that both martyr and playwright attended the same school. The young Blessed Robert travelled to Louvain in 1576 and, after making a pilgrimage to Rome, he arrived in Rheims on 29 December 1579, accompanying a priest back to England six months later. This was not a successful enterprise as both priest and Blessed Robert were arrested upon landing at Dover, being taken to the Gatehouse in Westminster. During his time in prison, Blessed Robert was fined four times for refusing to attend services of the Established Church.

Six months after being released in September 1582, Blessed Robert returned to the English College in Rheims, being ordained at the cathedral there on 31 March 1584. Back in England he ministered in the London area, including being involved in a series of exorcisms at Denham in Buckinghamshire that garnered attention from a wide spectrum of society.

Blessed Robert's arrest came from being recognised by pursuivants as he walked along Tothill Street in Westminster. Sent to the Counter prison at first, he was transferred to Newgate for trial along with Blessed John Lowe and Blessed John Adams, suffering and ultimately being beatified with them.

1587

BLESSED STEPHEN ROWSHAM

Born in Oxfordshire circa 1555
Hanged, drawn and quartered at Gloucester in
March 1587
Beatified by Pope St John Paul II on 22 November
1987

ALTHOUGH EDUCATED AT Oriel College, Oxford, Blessed Stephen Rowsham did not take his degree but he did take Anglican orders and served at St Mary's Oxford before being reconciled to the Catholic Church and then admitted to the English College in Rheims on St George's Day, 1581. He was ordained a priest at Soissons just five months later.

A year after having arrived at Rheims, Blessed George set out for England but was apprehended on landing and sent to the Tower of London, having to endure eighteen months captivity in the tiny cell notoriously and accurately referred to as 'Little Ease'. Not having betrayed any of his companions, he was banished in 1585 and, by 8 October, he had arrived back in Rheims where he recuperated for the next five months.

Determined to return to England, Blessed Stephen left Rheims on 7 February 1586 and, once back in England, was free to minister for a year until he was caught at the Gloucester home of a Mrs Strange, a lady known for caring for priests. Unlike his previous experience of prison, the officers of the prison at Gloucester seem to have treated the priest well, allowing him to celebrate Mass each day. But this was not to prevent the law taking its course and at the Lenten Assizes of 1587 Blessed Stephen was condemned to death. The previous priest to have been executed at Gloucester, Blessed John Sandys, had died such a terrible death due to the incompetence of the hangman that the authorities were careful to do all in their power for the death sentence to be executed as humanely as such a brutal death could possibly be.

BLESSED JOHN HAMBLEY

Born at St Mabyn, Cornwall circa 1560
Hanged, drawn and quartered at Salisbury March 1587
Beatified by Pope St John Paul II on 22 November 1987

BOOK WRITTEN BY Fr Robert Persons SJ was given to John Hambley at Christmas 1582: it was this that inspired him to become a Catholic. Realizing the danger of remaining in his home area if he did not attend the services of the Established Church, he travelled to London, making his home at the Sun and Seven Stars in

Smithfield, and was received into the Church by Father John Bollard in the Red Lion Inn at Holburn.

In early May Blessed John sailed from Rye in Sussex. Having landed in Dieppe he made his way to the English College in Rheims, being ordained a priest on 22 September 1584 at Laon. He remained abroad until returning to England in April of the following year. He landed on the coast of East Anglia and from there went to London where he and a fellow Cornishman, Blessed John Cornelius, briefly worked together on the mission. In May Blessed John left London for Devon, finding refuge in the home of a Catholic farmer near Beauminster. This was to be his base for a year until his capture on the road at Crewkerne in Somerset.

Having been imprisoned at Ilchester, Blessed John was tried and condemned to death at Taunton. Weakened by fear it seems that he may have spoken of considering recanting the Catholic Faith but, as he was not released, he almost certainly did not do this. But he did manage to escape, finding shelter in the house of a Mrs Browne at Knoyle in the south-west of Wiltshire where, soon enough, he was once more apprehended. Having been examined by the Bishop of Salisbury, John Piers, Blessed John agreed to renounce his faith, writing a long confession to this effect. But this did not stop his trial proceeding in Lent 1587 where, once again, he was condemned to death. Offered his life if he would once more embrace the Church of England, once again Blessed John's fear got the better of him and he agreed to accept the offer. According to one account, the next day in court he was publicly to confirm his decision when an unknown man approached him and gave him a letter. Upon reading the letter Blessed John burst into tears and renewed his profession of the Catholic Faith. Whatever the truth of 'the man with the letter' it is certain that a once fearful Blessed John was fortified by encouragement that he had received and prepared to die with new courage and strong faith.

BLESSED THOMAS PILCHER

Born at Battle, Sussex, in 1557
Hanged, drawn and quartered at Dorchester on 21 March 1587
Beatified by Pope St John Paul II on 22 November 1987

AVING RESIGNED HIS Fellowship of Baliol College, Oxford, in 1580, Blessed Thomas made his way to Rheims the following year, being ordained at Laon on 3 March 1583 and setting out for England on 4 May that year.

Unfortunately for Blessed Thomas, his squint made him quite easily recognizable, his former prominence at Baliol College probably not helping him remain totally unnoticed either. In 1585 he was caught in London and banished but he returned to England in January 1586 and was able to minister until March 1587 when he was once again caught, this time in Dorchester, and martyred. Accounts relate that during his time in prison Blessed Thomas continued his ministry reconciling many to the Faith, including a condemned man who was to executed with him. Blessed Thomas Pilcher is included among the names recorded at perhaps the most distinguished memorial to any of the English martyrs, the Dorset Martyrs Memorial by the sculptor Elisabeth Frink. The memorial, an ecumenical endeavour unveiled in 1986, honours the memory of all those who suffered for their faith in Dorset during the reformation.

BLESSED EDMUND SYKES

Born in Leeds, Yorkshire, circa 1550
Hanged, drawn and quartered at York on 23 March
1588
Beatified by Pope St John Paul II on 22 November
1987

UST OVER A year after enrolling as a student at the English College in Rheims, Blessed Edmund was ordained a priest on 21 February 1581, setting out for England in the following June. He was to be remembered in Yorkshire as living 'a very strict and straight life, wandering as a poor pilgrim, and coming to Leeds did help many with his holy life and doctrine.' But four years into his priestly life he was struck down with 'an extreme ague' and in this condition he was captured by Arthur Webster, a lapsed Catholic who hunted down priests. Blessed Edmund was taken to York and thrown into the notorious Kidcotes, a prison under Ousebridge, damp, dark and chilled by the proximity of the river. Already weak, this and examinations by officers weakened him further and he agreed to attend Protestant services. This saved his life—he was deported rather than executed—but plunged him into a spiritual depression.

With nine other exiled priests, Blessed Edmund was dispatched from Hull bound for Le Harve, then going on to Rheims. Having resolved to live the rest of his life in penance he went on pilgrimage to Rome to seek absolution, receiving there what he believed to be a divine revelation that told him that he had to return to England and face martyrdom there. This he resolved to do, travelling via Rheims, returning to Leeds.

He was able to minister for almost a year before he was betrayed by his very own brother in whose house he stayed near Tanfield in Wensleydale. At his trial the judge offered him his life should he recant once more, but this time Blessed Edmund stood firm, rejoicing and thanking God when his sentence was pronounced.

BLESSED ALEXANDER CROWE

Born at Howden, Yorkshire in 1550
Hanged, drawn and quartered at York on 30 November 1586 (or possibly 1587)
Beatified by Pope St John Paul II on 22 November 1987

IRST A COBBLER, then a porter, after that under-cook in the seminary and at last by his extreme diligence got as much learning as was sufficient for a priest'—thus Dr Humphrey Ely, a contemporary Douai student of Alexander Crowe, recalled this martyr's background. Blessed Alexander left his trade in York to travel to Rheims where ultimately he was ordained a priest on 17 December 1583. Within three months he had returned to England, working on the mission in East Yorkshire.

Crowe travelled around Yorkshire on foot, 'a man burning with zeal for souls, who therefore never refused any labour by which he could win them,' as his superior, Fr Richard Holtby SJ later recalled. Crowe's ministry was not to be a long one: he was captured in late 1586 whilst on his way to baptise a newly born child in South Duffield. In prison he was double fettered and contracted a fever that he was unable to rid himself of until death.

Despite suffering severely from fever Blessed Alexander was dragged from his bed to court in York. He went carrying a small wooden cross that he had made which was snatched from his hands and smashed by the gaolers. Not only did he not intend to hide his priesthood from the court but he was happy to proclaim it by shaving the crown of his head in the form of a priestly tonsure and welcoming the inevitable death sentence that was pronounced.

The night before his execution, whilst at prayer, it is recorded that Blessed Alexander experienced mystical visions, first of the devil and then the fortifying and comforting presence of the Blessed Virgin Mary and St John the Evangelist.

1588

BLESSED NICHOLAS GARLICK

Born near Glossop, Derbyshire, circa 1554
Hanged, drawn and quartered at St Mary's Bridge,
Derby, on 24 July 1588
Beatified by Pope St John Paul II on 22 November
1987

AFTER A FEW months at Gloucester College, Oxford, Blessed Nicholas spent seven years working as a schoolmaster at Tideswell, Derbyshire, counting among his pupils Robert Bagshaw, who was also to become a priest, writing an account of his former teacher's life, and the priest and martyr, Blessed Christopher Buxton, who quickly followed his former teacher in entering the English College. After one year of preparation, Blessed Nicholas was ordained a priest at Châlons-sur-Marne in March 1582, leaving the college for England the following January.

Between government spies and traitors, priests' lives were fraught with danger, a spy recording Blessed Nicholas's presence in Staffordshire in late 1584 after which he was arrested in London in 1585 and banished. After only two days in back in Rheims he set out once more for England. Over the next few years, government records note his presence in Hampshire and Dorset, one of Sir Francis Walsingham's spies bitterly noting that 'father Garlick the demonite ... laboureth with great diligence in Hampshire and Dorsetshire; would God he were intercepted.', the term 'demonite' certainly denoting exorcisms that Blessed Nicholas had executed.

It was in Derbyshire where he was finally arrested along with Blessed Robert Ludlam at the house of the Fitzherbert family in Padley, the principal pursuivant being George Talbot, Earl of Shrewsbury and Lord Lieutenant of Derbyshire. In prison the two priests met a third captured priest, Blessed Richard Simpson, with whom they went to the scaffold.

BLESSED ROBERT LUDLAM

Born in Radbourne, Derbyshire, circa 1551
Hanged, drawn and quartered at St Mary's Bridge, Derby, on 24 July 1588
Beatified by Pope St John Paul II on 22 November 1987

HAVING STUDIED FOR two years at St John's College, Oxford, and having worked as a teacher, Blessed Robert entered the English College in Rheims on 25 November 1580, being ordained a priest in September of the following year, setting out for England at the end of April 1582. An anonymous, but contemporary, chronicler wrote that Blessed Robert was 'beloved by all that loved the Catholic Church' and 'for that he did much travel'. That travel seems to have allowed him to allude government tracking until his arrest with Blessed

Nicholas Garlick at the house of John Fitzherbert. Fitzherbert, his own life now threatened, denied to the authorities that he knew that his guests were priests, the priests themselves corroborating this claim before they died. This saved John Fitzherbert's life, but not his freedom: after being held in Derby gaol for two years he was transferred to the Fleet in London, where he died in 1590.

BLESSED RICHARD SIMPSON

Born at Wall, near Bedale, circa 1553
Hanged, drawn and quartered at St Mary's Bridge,
Derby, on 24 July 1588
Beatified by Pope St John Paul II on 22 November
1987

BEFORE ARRIVING IN Douai in May 1577, Blessed Richard Simpson had already known the misery of imprisonment for his faith. In the same year that he enrolled in the college, he was ordained a priest in Brussels before being sent back to England—priestly studies of, at most, four months, such was the urgency of fielding priests in the English mission.

Having ministered in Derbyshire for the best part of ten years, Blessed Richard was arrested in the Peak District, tried and condemned to death.

Terrorized by what lay ahead, Blessed Richard weakened and undertook to attend Protestant services, but the judge was not convinced by his words and determined that he should be tried again. And while awaiting his retrial, he was joined in prison by Blessed Nicholas Garlick and Blessed Robert Ludlam who gave new courage to their brother priest. Blessed Richard greatly regretted his lack of constancy and strove to do penance for this until his death, it

being seen when his body was cut down after being hung,
that he wore a hair shirt. Challoner quotes a poem that may
have been written by an eyewitness to the death of the men
who have become known as the 'Padley Martyrs':

> When Garlick did the ladder kiss,
> And Sympson after hie,
> Methought that there St. Andrew was
> Desirous for to die.

> When Ludlam lookèd smilingly,
> And joyful did remain,
> It seemed St. Stephen was standing by,
> For to be stoned again.

> And what if Sympson seemed to yield,
> For doubt and dread to die;
> He rose again, and won the field
> And died most constantly.

> His watching, fasting, shirt of hair;
> His speech, his death, and all,
> Do record give, do witness bear,
> He wailed his former fall.

BLESSED ROBERT SUTTON

*Born in Burton-on-Trent, Staffordshire, in 1544
Hanged, drawn and quartered in Stafford on 27 July
1588
Beatified by Pope St John Paul II on 22 November 1987*

HE SON OF a carpenter, Blessed Robert was the
eldest of three brothers who became Catholics
and, in due course, were ordained priests. Robert
was a member of Christ Church College, Oxford, between

1561 and 1571. He took Anglican orders and became the Rector of Lutterworth, Leicestershire, where he ministered for five years. Increasingly he was influenced by one of his younger brothers, William, who had already become a Catholic and entered Douai. With his other brother, Abraham, Blessed Robert also converted, entering Douai together on 23 March 1577, being able to attend their elder brother's priestly ordination. Robert and Abraham were ordained priests on 23 February 1578, leaving for England a few weeks later.

For ten years Blessed Robert eluded the government's clutches, but not their notice. He seems to have ministered mostly in Staffordshire but in 1584 a spy claimed that he had said Mass a number of times in a house on Fleet Street, London. He was finally tracked down on 18 July 1588 along with seven other Catholics, according to one account, while he was saying Mass. At trial the lay Catholics were found guilty of harbouring a priest but were allowed to pay fines rather than face more extreme censure. After his execution, not all of Blessed Robert's body was lost after a year of decay 'pinned up to be eaten by birds', his right thumb, 'set in gold', and index finger being among the arsenal of relics held by the recusant Vaux family. Significant relics these, as Fr John Gerard was to note, as these digits had been 'anointed with sacred oil at ordination' and sanctified by the touch of the Blessed Sacrament'.

BLESSED WILLIAM DEAN

Born in Grassington, Yorkshire, date of birth unknown
Hanged, drawn and quartered at Mile End, London,
on 28 August 1588
Beatified by Pope Pius XI on 15 December 1929

AGDALENE AND CAIUS Colleges, Cambridge, educated Blessed William who went on to become a
minister of the Established Church at Monk
Fryston in the Diocese of York before becoming a Catholic,
being received into the Church by Blessed Thomas Alfield
in 1581, setting out for Rheims and being ordained a priest
at Soissons on 21 December of the very same year along
with the *beati* George Haydock and Robert Nutter.

Within a month of arriving back in England, Blessed
William was arrested on 21 February 1582 and imprisoned
at Newgate and tortured by Topcliffe, a name that was to
become synonymous with cruelty and corruption. He was
held for two years before being transferred to the Clink
where he was incarcerated until he and twenty other
priests were banished in early 1585. By the end of that year
he was back but, again, swiftly apprehended and then sent
to the Gatehouse prison where he was held until his trial
and condemnation, along with thirteen others, on 22
August 1588. At his martyrdom, as he attempted to speak
someone hit him so hard on the head that, in Challoner's
words, 'they were like to have prevented the hangman of
his wages.' Also martyred with Blessed William was
Blessed Henry Webley, a layman who had been reconciled
to the Church and who had assisted the priest.

BLESSED WILLIAM GUNTER

Born in Raglan, Monmouthshire, date of birth unknown
Hanged, drawn and quartered at Lincoln's Inn
Fields, London, on 28 August 1588
Beatified by Pope Pius XI on 15 December 1929

LMOST NOTHING IS known of this martyr's life except his origins, that he was ordained a priest in 1587 after some study at the English College in Rheims and that he suffered on the same day as twenty-one other priests.

BLESSED ROBERT MORTON

Born in Bawtry, Yorkshire, in 1548
Hanged, drawn and quartered at Lincoln's Inn
Fields, London, on 28 August 1588
Beatified by Pope Pius XI on 15 December 1929

LESSED ROBERT'S UNCLE, Fr Nicholas Morton, was a considerable influence on this priest and martyr. Blessed Robert would have remembered him, 'a most loving uncle', before he fled to Rome in 1561 'having', as a memorial plaque paid for by Blessed Robert and set up in the church of the English College in Rome records, 'lost his dearest friends and all other goods in his native country for the sake of the Catholic Faith'. His uncle died on 27 January 1587 during a visit of his nephew to Rome: the memorial can still be seen on the sacristy side of the English College Chapel. On 5 April 1587 Blessed

Robert took the college oath and received all the orders as far as diaconate within just one month.

Leaving Rome, he and five others travelled to the college in Rheims where he was ordained a priest on 14 June, being sent to England on 2 July. He was quickly apprehended. There is no doubt that this priest would have held considerable interest for the government given that his priestly uncle had encouraged the pope to publicly excommunicate Queen Elizabeth and another uncle had been involved with the Northern Uprising of 1569. It can be assumed that Blessed Robert was ruthlessly tortured in the hope of extracting information about Rome and home during his imprisonment.

BLESSED HUGH MORE

Born in Grantham, Lincolnshire, date of birth unknown
Hanged, drawn and quartered at Lincoln's Inn Fields, London, on 28 August 1588
Beatified by Pope Pius XI on 15 December 1929

SON OF A Grantham landowner, Blessed Hugh was possibly educated at Oxford and Gray's Inn before arriving in the English College, Rheims, and being ordained a priest, returning to England where he was quickly captured, tried and executed.

BLESSED THOMAS HOLFORD

Born in Cheshire in 1541
Hanged, drawn and quartered at Clerkenwell,
London, on 28 August 1588
Beatified by Pope Pius XI on 15 December 1929

HE SON OF a minister, Blessed Thomas became a schoolmaster and, before his embracing the Catholic faith, was tutor to the children of Sir James Scudamore of Hole Lacy. About 1579 Blessed Thomas was received into the Church, having been instructed by Fr Richard Davis, a priest who was to leave an account of Holford's life. On 18 August 1582 the future martyr was admitted to the English College at Rheims, being ordained a priest at Laon on 9 April the following year and setting out for England the next month.

He narrowly escaped capture near Harrow-on-the-Hill on All Souls' Day 1584 but was less fortunate in May 1585 when he was arrested in Nantwich. He was examined by the Bishop of Chester who recorded a description of the captive's appearance: 'tall, black (haired), fat, strong man, the crown of his head bald, his beard marquessated [shaven except for a moustache]'. Blessed Thomas refused the option of exile, stating that he was ready to die, and was sent to London but manged to escape his captors by feigning insanity when they were drunk.

In 1586 Blessed Thomas again escaped the clutches of the pursuivants and left London. It was when returning to the city to buy clothes that he was recognised leaving the house of St Swithun Wells having just said Mass. Unaware of the immediate danger he made his way to a tailor where he was arrested and taken to Newgate prison.

Blessed James Claxton

Born in Yorkshire, date of birth unknown
Hanged, drawn and quartered at Bush Corner, near
Brentford, on 28 August 1588
Beatified by Pope Pius XI on 15 December 1929

FTER HIS ORDINATION at Soissons on 9 June 1582 very little is known of the life of Blessed James Claxton. He was among a group of priests who were captured and banished in 1585. Upon returning he was rearrested and taken to the Marshalsea, being martyred with Blessed Thomas Felton.

Blessed Thomas Felton

Born in Bermondsey Abbey, Surrey, circa 1566
Hanged, drawn and quartered at Bush Corner, near
Brentford, on 28 August 1588
Beatified by Pope Pius XI on 15 December 1929

RAZEN BRAVERY CHARACTERISED Blessed Thomas's father, the martyr John Felton, and must have stiffened the resolve of this the priest who followed in his father's steps to martyrdom. On 25 May 1570 John Felton had nailed a copy of Pope St Pius V's bull *Regnans in excelsis*, the decree that declared Elizabeth I excommunicated, to the door of the Bishop of London's palace next to St Paul's Cathedral. He was proud to profess that he had done so, was racked at the Tower in the hope of extracting utterances that would implicate others, arraigned at the Guildhall and finally taken back to the place where he had published and therefore promulgated the papal bull, St Paul's Cathedral Churchyard, to be hanged, drawn and quartered by—and how his oppressors enjoyed this—an executioner called Bull.

While he would have had no memory of his father, being about two years old at the time of his death, it can well be imagined that Blessed Thomas heard him being praised and admired as he grew up. Very young, he was sent to the English College at Rheims, receiving his clerical tonsure from Cardinal Louis de Guise, Archbishop of Rheims, in 1583. Whilst at Rheims he was admitted to the order of Minims but, either for reasons of health or family, he returned to England soon afterwards. His attempt to return to Rheims was thwarted by being arrested and imprisoned in the Poultry compter for two years. An aunt managed to secure his release and once again he set out for Rheims but once again he was arrested, this time being sent to the Bridewell prison. Lady Elizabeth Lovel, a gentlewoman to whom Blessed Thomas had acted as a page in his youth, was able to gain his release despite being herself held a prisoner due to her recusancy. Yet again Blessed Thomas attempted to reach Rheims but was apprehended and taken to Bridewell prison where he was mercilessly tortured but held fast to the Catholic faith. Although his family had secured the possibility of him being pardoned, the pardon was conditional upon clauses that were unacceptable to him, almost certainly with regard to the queen being head of the church in England. Like father, like son, Blessed Thomas was martyred for his faith.

BLESSED RICHARD LEIGH

Born in London in 1561
Hanged, drawn and quartered at Tyburn, London,
on 30 August 1588
Beatified by Pope Pius XI on 15 December 1929

F THE FIVE men martyred at Tyburn on 30 August 1588, only Blessed Richard Leigh was a priest, the other four—the beati Edward Shelly, Richard Martin, John Roche and Richard Lloyd—were all laymen who were sentenced to death for harbouring or assisting priests: a powerful reminder that hundreds of good men and women risked their lives for the Faith during the years of greatest persecution.

Blessed Richard first entered Douai College at Rheims in 1581 before being sent to the English College, Rome, the following year, being ordained a priest in Rome in 1586. Back in England his ministry was to last but two years before he was arrested and imprisoned in the Tower of London on 4 July having attempted to enter into disputation with the Bishop of London who referred to the priest as 'a papist dog and traitor'.

Blessed William Way

Born in Devon or Cornwall circa 1562
Hanged, drawn and quartered in Kingston-on-Thames on 23 September 1588
Beatified by Pope Pius XI on 15 December 1929

Ordained at Laon on 20 September 1586, by the end of the year Blessed William was working in the London area, but not for long. He was arrested in Lambeth in the middle of 1587 and thrown into the Clink Street prison in Southwark. Blessed William not only declined to be tried by a secular judge but also made clear to the Bishop of London, who was then to take charge of his proceedings, that in no way did he consider that the man was a real bishop. Reputed to have been an austere man, Blessed William's joy at his fate is recorded in the chronicles of the martyrs.

Blessed Robert Wilcox

Born in Chester in 1558
Hanged, drawn and quartered at Canterbury on 1 October 1588
Beatified by Pope Pius XI on 15 December 1929

THE FIRST OF four to be martyred at Oaten Hill, Canterbury, on 1 October 1588 was Blessed Robert Wilcox who had been ordained a priest on 20 April 1585 after studies in Rheims. The following year he arrived in Kent but was arrested almost immediately at Lydd, near to where he had landed. Sent to the

Marshalsea in London he was returned to Canterbury after examination for trial and martyrdom.

BLESSED EDWARD CAMPION

Born in Ludlow, Shropshire, circa 1552
Hanged, drawn and quartered at Canterbury on 1
October 1588
Beatified by Pope Pius XI on 15 December 1929

DMIRATION FOR THE recently martyred St Edmund Campion inspired Gerard Edwards to take up the alias of Edward Campion on entering Douai College at Rheims in 1586. Having come from a gentry family and studied at Oxford (Jesus College— though he did not take his degree due to being unable to agree to make the necessary Oath of Supremacy) Blessed Edward certainly had much in common with his hero.

Having been ordained a priest, Blessed Edward returned to England around Easter 1587 but remained free to minister for only a few weeks before he was arrested at Sittingbourne, Kent, and taken to the Marshalsea and then Newgate for interrogation. During his second examination in August1587 he admitted to being a priest and was sent on to Canterbury for trial and the ensuing inevitable execution.

BLESSED CHRISTOPHER BUXTON

Born in Derbyshire in 1562
Hanged, drawn and quartered at Canterbury on
1 October 1588
Beatified by Pope Pius XI on 15 December 1929

Educated by Blessed Nicholas Garlick at the grammar school
of Tideswell, in the Peak District, Blessed Christopher
followed his tutor to Rheims in the early summer of 1581.
Three years later he was sent to the English College in Rome
to finish preparation for priesthood and was ordained at the
Lateran Basilica on 26 October 1586. At first advised to hold
back from returning to England, Blessed Christopher determined to cross the channel to Kent in early September 1587:
within two months he had been caught and taken to the
Marshalsea. Set to be the third priest to die at Canterbury
on the day of execution, the authorities hoped that having
witnessed the horror of the first two deaths he might relent
and recant his faith, but to this offer he replied, 'that he would
not purchase a corruptible life at such a rate, and that if he
had a hundred lives he would willingly lay them all down in
defence of his faith'. After the three priests had been martyred a Nottinghamshire born layman, Blessed Robert Wid-
merpool, also gave his life for the Faith, having been found
guilty of harbouring priests.

BLESSED RALPH CROKETT

Born in Barton, Cheshire, in 1550
Hanged, drawn and quartered at Chichester on 1
October 1588
Beatified by Pope Pius XI on 15 December 1929

OUR PRIESTS WERE arraigned in Chichester on 30 September 1588 and condemned to death, two of which persevered in the Faith until the end: Blessed Ralph Crokett and Blessed Edward James.

Blessed Ralph was educated at Christ's College, Cambridge, after which he became a schoolmaster in Norfolk. He continued his studies at Gloucester Hall, Oxford (then belonging to St John's College before becoming Worcester College), before teaching for five years in Ipswich after which he moved to Cheshire.

In 1584 Blessed Ralph began studies at Douai College, then in Rheims, being ordained a priest in 1585. Together with three other priests, including Blessed Edward James, Blessed Ralph set out for England in April 1586. They crossed to England from Dieppe but their ship ran ashore at Littlehampton, Sussex, on 19 April and all four priests were arrested and sent to the Marshalsea.

It can only be surmised that between capture and trial, a period of over two years, Blessed Ralph and Edward were very probably tortured as they remained in prison. They were tried together with Fr John Oven and Fr Francis Edwardes at Chichester on 30 September 1588. All were sentenced to death, but Oven immediately abjured his faith and took the Oath of Supremacy, thereby saving his life. The day after their trial the remaining three priests were all drawn on a single hurdle to Broyle Heath, just outside Chichester, where they were to be executed. This was all too much for Edwardes who recanted his faith and was reprieved. The two remaining priest martyrs gave each other absolution before making the ultimate sacrifice. Before dying, Blessed Ralph blessed the crowd in Latin, drawing shouts of anger and derision. He then changed to English: the crowd cheered. After their deaths, the quartered bodies of the martyrs were set up over the gates of the city though one of these quarters fell down and was retrieved by a Catholic man who was passing by early in the morning 'which,' relates Challoner, 'by the size, was judged to be Mr. Crokett's (he having been a tall man, whereas Mr. James was of low stature). This quarter was carried off and sent over to Douai, where I have seen it.' The martyr's father, once safely abroad, also became a Catholic in his later years.

BLESSED EDWARD JAMES

Born in Breaston, Derbyshire, date of birth unknown
Hanged, drawn and quartered at Chichester on 1
October 1588
Beatified by Pope Pius XI on 15 December 1929

REFUSING TO TAKE the oath of supremacy, Blessed Edward was not awarded his degree after his four years at St John's College, Oxford. In 1579 he entered the college in Rheims before being sent on to the English College in Rome where he was ordained on 30 October 1583, leaving the Eternal City almost two years later. He did not even take a single step on English soil as a free man, being apprehended before having the opportunity of leaving the ship that he and Blessed Ralph

Crokett had hoped would bring them safely home rather
than be his passage to two years at the Clink in London,
trial and martyrdom at Chichester.

BLESSED JOHN ROBINSON

Born in North Riding of Yorkshire, date of birth unknown
Hanged, drawn and quartered at Ipswich on 1 October
1588
Beatified by Pope Pius XI on 15 December 1929

Marriage was the first vocation of Blessed John Robinson,
a son, Francis, being born to him and his wife in 1569.
Upon his wife's death, Blessed John entered the college at
Rheims, returning to England briefly in August 1584 to
visit his son. In April of the next year he was ordained a
priest, returning to England two months later. Having
arrived safely he took a ship that was setting sail for the
north of England but the vessel put in at Great Yarmouth
and he was arrested, being sent to the Clink where he was
imprisoned for three years before trial and execution. As
he awaited trial, some accounts relate that Blessed John
would say that 'If he could not dispute for his faith as well
as some others, he could die for it as well as the best.' His
son, Francis, was ordained a priest five years after his holy
father's death.

BLESSED WILLIAM HARTLEY

Born at Wyn, Derbyshire, circa 1557
Hanged, drawn and quartered at Shoreditch, London, on
5 October 1588
Beatified by Pope Pius XI on 15 December 1929

In 1579 Blessed William Hartley was removed from his post as chaplain at St John's College, Oxford, being suspected of Catholic tendencies. The suspicions were well founded as Blessed William headed off to the English College at Rheims, being ordained a priest at Châlons on 24 February 1580, setting out for England in June of that year.

Part of his mission in England was assisting St Edmund Campion and Fr Robert Persons in printing and distributing their books. A search of Stonor Park, Oxfordshire, in August 1581 found the press being employed and Blessed William and members of the Stonor family and their household were arrested, the priest being sent to the Marshalsea prison in London where, to the best of his ability, he continued to minister among the prisoners. But he was detected saying Mass before Lord Vaux in his cell and Blessed William suffered for his care by being clapped in irons. Having been accused of being part of a conspiracy against the crown, despite having been imprisoned at the time, he was banished from the realm. He used his time of exile to regain strength of health and make a pilgrimage to Rome in April 1586 after which he returned to England being arrested for the final time in September 1588. Challoner relates that the martyr's mother witnessed his death, 'rejoicing exceedingly that she had brought forth a son to glorify God by such a death.'.

BLESSED JOHN HEWITT

Born in York, date of birth unknown
Hanged, drawn and quartered at Mile End, London,
on 5 October 1588
Beatified by Pope Pius XI on 15 December 1929

HE SON OF a draper and an alumnus of Caius College, Cambridge, Blessed John had returned to England as a deacon, probably due to ill health, and was apprehended in York: he was among those who were banished in 1585. Back in Rheims he was ordained a priest and set out for England in January 1586 under the alias 'Weldon' and disguised as a servant of John Gardiner Esq of Buckinghamshire. Possibly the following year he was arrested at Gardiner's lodgings in Gray's Inn Lane, London, and sent to Newgate to await trial and, ultimately, death.

BLESSED EDWARD BURDEN

Born in Co. Durham circa 1540
Hanged, drawn and quartered at York circa 29
November 1588
Beatified by Pope St John Paul II on 22 November 1987

N 1561 BLESSED Edward became a Fellow of his Cambridge college, Corpus Christi, receiving his MA in December 1566. He was admitted to the English College at Rheims on 24 June 1583 and was ordained a priest at Soissons on 13 June the following year. Poor health prevented his immediate return to England thus it was to be on 22 May 1586 that he set out for England, ministering in the area of York and Ripon.

Dogged by his poor health, Blessed Edward retreated from pressures of the mission in early 1588, finding, he had hoped, a safe place of rest in the hamlet of Skinningrove on the north coast of Yorkshire. But being a stranger in those parts, led him to be closely questioned by one Mr John Constable and then arrested by him. Taken to York and imprisoned in the castle, his health further deteriorated leaving him a weak man at his trial and death.

1589

BLESSED ROBERT DALBY

Born at Hemingbrough, Yorkshire, date of birth unknown

BLESSED JOHN AMIAS

Born at Wakefield, Yorkshire, date of birth unknown

Both hanged, drawn and quartered at York on 16 March 1589
Beatified by Pope Pius XI on 15 December 1929

BLESSED ROBERT LEFT ministry in the Church of England to become a Catholic, entering the English College at Rheims on 30 September 1586. He was ordained a priest at Châlons on 16 April 1588, setting out for England on 25 August of the same year. He was arrested almost directly upon landing at Scarborough and imprisoned in York Castle.

It is thought that Blessed John was a widower with children who traded as a clothmaker. Upon the death of his wife he made his way to the English College at Rheims which he entered on 22 June 1580 being ordained a priest on 25 March 1581 at Rheims Cathedral. He travelled to England via Paris along with another priest, Blessed Edmund Sykes. After some years of missionary work Blessed John was seized at the house of Mr Murton at Melling in Lancashire and then imprisoned in York Castle. Both Blessed John and Blessed Robert were executed together and there exists an eyewitness account from the priest and writer Dr Champney of their martyrdom:

> This year, on 16th of March, John Amias and Robert Dalby, priests of the College of Douay, suffered at York as in cases of high treason, for no other cause but that they were priests ordained by the authority of the See of Rome, and had returned into England, and exercised there their priestly functions for the benefit of the souls of their neighbours. I was myself an eyewitness of the glorious combat of these holy men, being at that time a young man in the twentieth year of my age; and I returned home confirmed by the sight of their constancy and meekness in the Catholic faith, which by God's grace I then followed. For there visibly appeared in these holy servants of God such meekness, joined with singular constancy, that you would easily say that they were lambs led to the slaughter.

> They were drawn about a mile out of the city to the place of execution, where being arrived and taken off the hurdle, they prostrated themselves upon their faces to the ground, and there employed some time in prayer, till the former, [Mr. Amias,] being called upon by the Sheriff, rose up, and with a serene

countenance walked to the gallows and kissed it, then
kissing the ladder, went up. The hangman having
fitted the rope to his neck, bid him descend a step or
two lower, affirming that by this means he would
suffer the less. He then turned to the people, declared,
that the cause of his death was not treason, but
religion. But here he was interrupted, and not suffered to go on. Therefore composing himself for
death, with his eyes and hands lifted up to heaven,
forgiving all who had any ways procured his death,
and praying for his persecutors, he recommended his
soul to God; and being flung off the ladder, quietly
expired: for he was suffered to hang so long till he
seemed to be quite dead. Then he was cut down,
dismembered, and bowelled, his bowels cast into a
fire that was prepared hard by for that purpose, his
head cut off, and the trunk of his body quartered. All
this while his companion, Mr Dalby, was most intent
on prayer; who being called upon, immediately
followed the footsteps of him that gone before him,
and obtained the like victory. The Sheriff's men were
very watchful to prevent the standers by from gathering any of their blood, or carrying off anything that
had belonged to them. Yet one, who appeared to me
to be a gentlewoman, going up to the place where
their bodies were in quartering, and not without
difficulty making her way through the crowd, fell
down upon her knees before the multitude. And, with
her hands joined and eyes lifted up to heaven,
declared an extraordinary motion and affection of
soul. She spoke also some words, which I could not
hear for the tumult and noise. Immediately a clamour
was raised against her as an idolatress, and she was
drove away; and whether or no she was carried to
prison, I could not certainly understand.

BLESSED GEORGE NICHOLS

Born at Oxford circa 1550
Hanged, drawn and quartered at Oxford on 5 July 1589
Beatified by Pope St John Paul II on 22 November 1987

AVING GRADUATED FROM Brasenose College, Oxford, in 1571 Blessed George Nichols worked as an assistant master at St Paul's School, London, before being received into the Catholic Church. He entered the English College at Rheims in November 1581, was ordained a priest in Rheims Cathedral on 24 September 1583 and travelled to England sometime during the next year. Having made his way to Oxford Blessed George commenced his ministry, audaciously and secretly visiting the prison there.

Such brazen bravery along with persistent activity ultimately came to the attention of the Privy Council who, in 1589, ordered a search for priests in Oxford. Led by the Constable of Oxford, a group of pursuivants raided the Catherine Wheel Inn, a hostelry suspected of being a centre of Catholic activities. During the raid not only were the priests Blessed George and Blessed Richard Yaxley detained but Mass vestments were also discovered, confirming the constable's suspicions that clandestine Masses were being held at the inn. Two laymen, both who were to join the priests in their ultimate fate and heavenly reward, were also arrested during the raid: Blessed Humphrey Prichard and Blessed Thomas Belson.

Blessed George made no attempt to hide his priesthood when brought before the Court of the Chancellor of the University. As the Privy Council had instigated the investigation into Catholic life in Oxford, all four detainees were sent to London for further questioning. Despite torture, Blessed George withheld any information that he had about other Catholics in Oxford. When no more torture was deemed to be worthwhile, the two priests and the two laymen were sent back to Oxford for trial, condemnation and death, Blessed George being the first to die on the scaffold after professing his faith. With these martyrs died the highwayman, Harcourt, whom Blessed George had reconciled to the Faith while in prison.

BLESSED RICHARD YAXLEY

Born at Boston, Lincolnshire circa 1560
Hanged, drawn and quartered at Oxford on 5 July 1589
Beatified by Pope St John Paul II on 22 November 1987

ORN OF A well to do family, Blessed Richard entered the English College at Rheims in August 1582, being ordained a priest in the Cathedral of Rheims on 21 September 1585 and leaving the College for England on 28 January the following year. At first, he ministered in and around Denham, Buckinghamshire, before moving to the environs of Oxford where he joined with a fellow priest, Blessed George Nichols, in the work of the mission. Both priests were arrested during a pursuivants' raid of the Catherine Wheel Inn, Magdalen Street, in 1589.

Only upon being transferred to London and given into the hands of the torturers did Blessed Richard confess that he was a priest. He was taken to the Tower of London, denied any visitors except the notoriously cruel torturer,

Richard Topcliffe. Subsequently he was returned to Oxford with Blessed George Nichols and the two laymen who had been arrested with them. Having been condemned to death, they were all executed at the Holywell Gallows. Blessed Richard was the second to die that day, embracing the body of Blessed George Nichols and asking for his intercession before he faced death himself. The heads of the priests were displayed on Oxford Castle, their four quarters being hung on the four city gates. Today a plaque on the wall of 100 Holywell Street (the nearest house to where the Holywell Gallows stood) records their sacrifice, as does a further plaque in the University Church of Oxford that records all those of the city who died for their faith during the reformation.

BLESSED THOMAS BELSON

Born in Aston Rowant, Oxfordshire, in 1563
Hanged at Oxford on 5 July 1589
Beatified by Pope St John Paul II on 22 November 1987

HE YOUNGEST CHILD of a wealthy landowner, Augustine Belson, and his wife Margaret, Blessed Thomas was born into what had become a defiant recusant family. Augustine Belson's recusancy was all the more noticeable as he had been churchwarden at Aston Rowant and therefore, to avoid the substantial fines, he had passed over ownership of most of his land to his three sons. In 1575 the family moved to Ixhill Lodge in Buckinghamshire, an area where the magistrates were more lenient towards Catholic families but not so lenient as to turn a blind eye to Catholic services at the Belson home which was raided a number of times, on one occasion the priest escaping but a box with a false bottom being discovered revealing items used for saying Mass.

Although nothing is known of Blessed Thomas's early education, an inventory of his belongings included both a Greek new testament and a Hebrew psalter, a family commonplace book also contained a Latin sonnet that he had drafted. At the age of sixteen he matriculated from St Mary's Hall, Oxford, supplicating three years later for his BA but never receiving it as he would not take the oath of supremacy.

His father's financial astuteness was inherited by Blessed Thomas for before setting out to the English College at Rheims he transferred most of his properties to his brother, William, to avoid the penalty of confiscation of all his possessions that he would have incurred had it been discovered, as it would have been, that he was studying abroad. He remained at Douai College for one year, leaving the college as a layman in April 1584. Nothing further is known of Blessed Thomas until his arrest and imprisonment in the Tower of London in June 1585, having been accused of assisting St Philip Howard, Earl of Arundel, in his attempt to leave the country. In November 1586 Blessed Thomas was banished from the country but was still in the Tower four months later, being released at some point after this.

At midnight on 18 May 1589 Blessed Thomas was arrested at the Catherine Wheel Inn in Oxford together with the Douai priests Blessed George Nichols and Blessed Richard Yaxley and a servant at the inn, Blessed Humphrey Prichard. Six weeks of torture and interrogation in London ensued before the four were sent back to Oxford for trial and condemnation—going to London they were taken on horseback, for the return to Oxford they were carried in a wagon, the torture having rendered them incapable of riding again. Blessed Thomas was hanged as a felon after the priests, first embracing their butchered bodies and thanking God that he was able to appear before Him in such good company.

Blessed William Spencer

Born in Gisburn, West Riding of Yorkshire, circa 1555
Hanged, drawn and quartered at York on 24 September
1589
Beatified by Pope St John Paul II on 22 November 1987

FELLOW OF TRINITY College, Oxford, in 1582 Blessed William left the dreaming spires for the continent, embarking from the Isle of Wight, landing in Cherbourg and going on to Rheims with four other Trinity men to become Catholics and to study for the priesthood. He was ordained at Rheims on 24 September 1583, returning to England just under a year later.

One of the four Oxford men who had travelled with Blessed William to Rheims, William Warfield, wrote an account of his friend and martyr. In it he notes that Blessed William's first concern was to reconcile his parents to the Faith and then his uncle, a Protestant minister. His parents had sent him to his uncle to be educated as a young man fully knowing that he was himself most sympathetic to the Catholic Faith, as were they. With their reconciliation accomplished, Warfield writes, 'he began more freely and boldly to expose himself to danger and to work more earnestly in order to help souls'. In particular, Blessed William became concerned for the plight of Catholic prisoners held in York Castle and so he managed to get himself a hiding place within the castle so that he could be amongst them and offer them the Sacraments.

On 1 August 1589, on the road to Ripon, Blessed William was arrested along with Blessed Robert Hardesty, a layman who gave him shelter. Both were taken to York and, after trial, were executed together, six years to the day since Blessed William's ordination, and, according to a witness, 'he took his death merrily'.

1590

BLESSED CHRISTOPHER BALES

Born in Coniscliffe, Durham, in March 1564
Hanged, drawn and quartered in Fleet Street,
London on 4 March 1590
Beatified by Pope Pius XI on 15 December 1929

ROUGHT UP AS a Protestant, Blessed Christopher entered the college at Rheims having become a Catholic on 10 June 1581, continuing his studies at the English College, Rome, from 1 October of the following year. Ill health caused him to return to Rheims just one year later, being ordained a priest at Laon on 28 March 1587, having obtained a dispensation as he was under the canonical age for ordination.

On All Souls' Day 1588 he began his journey to England, sailing across the channel with Blessed Edward Oldcorne and Fr John Gerard. He probably ministered in the Gray's Inn area where he lodged, for this was where he was caught on the Feast of the Assumption the very next year, being sent to the Bridewell prison where he received the unwelcome attention of Topcliffe, Blessed Christopher being the subject of the first of many warrants for torture that Topcliffe was to receive. The torture—being racked and being suspended by his wrists for a whole day and night— could not procure from the priest any information as to in whose homes he had celebrated Mass during his time in England.

One account relates that upon being given the chance to speak at his trial he asked the court if they thought that St Augustine of Canterbury, having been sent to England to evangelize by Pope St Gregory the Great, had committed treason. Unsurprisingly the court declared that this had not been the case, causing Blessed Christopher to respond that if this was so then, why was it deemed different for him? The response was the simple stating that such acts were now treason by the law of the land. Two others were hanged on the same day as the execution of Blessed Christopher: Blessed Nicholas Horner, a tailor who had been in prison before for assisting priests, needing to have one of his legs amputated and thus released but, as far as the court was concerned, reoffending by giving Blessed Christopher Bales a jerkin; and Blessed Alexander Blake, who looked after horses at inns, in whose house at Gray's Inn Lane Blessed Christopher had been given lodging. Both were hanged outside their front doors, the former in Smithfield, the latter in Gray's Inn Lane.

Blessed Francis Dickenson

Born in Otley, West Riding of Yorkshire, in 1565

Blessed Miles Gerard

Born in Wigan, Lancashire, in 1549, date of birth unknown

Both hanged, drawn and quartered at Rochester, Kent, on 19 or 30 April 1590
Beatified by Pope Pius XI on 15 December 1929

LESSED FRANCIS WAS a very young man when he entered the college at Rheims circa 1582, Blessed Miles being enrolled in 1580. The former was ordained at Soissons 18 March 1589, the latter ordained 7 April 1583 but remaining at the college as a professor until the end of August 1589 when the two priests, along with three others, set out for England. Arriving at the French coast, the captain of the ship would only accept two of the men and Blessed Francis and Miles were chosen by lot. The weather being stormy, the voyage was a terrible experience and ended with the vessel being shipwrecked on the English coast, local people raiding the wreck and taking the passengers to Dover where they were expected to swear the oath of supremacy. Both refusing to take the oath and both giving aliases rather than stating their true names, the priests were taken to London for examination. Under interrogation and torture both admitted to being priests and were held in prison until April 1590 when they

were returned to Rochester for martyrdom, Blessed
Francis having been a priest for little over one year.

BLESSED EDWARD JONES

*Born in Llanelidan, North Wales, date of birth
unknown*
*Hanged, drawn and quartered in Fleet Street,
London, 6 May 1590*
Beatified by Pope Pius XI on 15 December 1929

HAVING BEEN RECEIVED into the Catholic Church
in 1587, Blessed Edward Jones was ordained a
priest on 11 June 1588. At the end of that year he
returned to England finding lodging in a grocer's shop in
Fleet Street, London. He was very quickly apprehended
there by the notorious Richard Topcliffe and, under torture
in the Tower of London, admitted to being a priest. After
trial at the Old Bailey, Jones was executed in Fleet Street,
opposite the very grocers where he had been lodging. Over
the gallows was written the charge, 'For treason and favour-
ing of foreign invasion.' As he objected to this he was
thrown off the scaffold, the butchery having begun.

BLESSED ANTONY MIDDLETON

Born in Yorkshire, date of birth unknown
Hanged, drawn and quartered in Clerkenwell,
London, 6 May 1590
Beatified by Pope Pius XI on 15 December 1929

AFTER STUDIES AT Rheims and ordination as a priest, Blessed Antony Middleton landed in England in 1586 it being held that his small stature and appearing younger than his years helped him to avoid suspicion of being a priest until the government spies caught up with him. Like Blessed Edward Jones, Middleton was executed outside the house where he had been arrested. Not being allowed to address those present at his martyrdom, he was able to simply state that he was dying for the Catholic Faith and for being a priest, praying that his death would be accepted by God as expiation for his sins and would bring others to the true Faith.

BLESSED EDMUND DUKE

Born in Kent in 1563

BLESSED RICHARD HILL

Born in Yorkshire, date of birth unknown

BLESSED JOHN HOGG

Born in Ugthorpe, Cleveland, date of birth unknown

BLESSED RICHARD HOLIDAY

Born in Yorkshire, date of birth unknown

All four hanged, drawn and quartered at Durham on 27 May 1590 and beatified by Pope St John Paul II on 22 November 1987

HAVING BECOME A Catholic, Blessed Edmund first prepared for priesthood at Rheims before being sent on to the English College, Rome. He was ordained in the Basilica of St John Lateran on 3 September 1589. His journey back to England was via Rheims, where three other priests trained in Rheims, of whom almost nothing is known—the beati Richard Hill, John Hogg and Richard Holiday—joined him on his homeward journey. Landing near Tynemouth, plans that had carefully been made for their safe reception were thrown into disarray by the recent success of the pursuivants and the four were swiftly betrayed as they looked for refuge in a nearby village. They were taken to Durham gaol and a mere two months after having left Rheims, they were martyred together in Durham and are now known locally as the Dryburn Martyrs, named after the site of their execution. The burial register of St Oswald's Church, Durham, records the burial of four priests in 1590.

1591

BLESSED ROBERT THORPE

Born in Yorkshire, date of birth unknown
Hanged, drawn and quartered at York on 31 May
1591
Beatified by Pope St John Paul II on 22 November 1987

ADMITTED TO THE English College at Rheims on 1 May 1584, Blessed Robert was ordained a priest the following year on 6 April at the cathedral of Rheims. Returning to England, he ministered in the East Riding of Yorkshire, frequently visiting the Babthorpes at Osgodby Hall, Lady Grace Babthorpe describing her priest as 'of low stature, of infirm health, of mediocre learning, but of great devotion and piety'.

In the early hours of Palm Sunday, 28 March 1591, Blessed Robert was arrested at the house of Blessed Thomas Watkinson, the priest's attempt to quietly slip into the village having been noticed the night before. Both men were imprisoned in York but for reasons unknown Richard Topcliffe took a particular interest in the case of Blessed Robert, having him brought to London for interrogation and torture and accompanying him back to York, sitting with the Council of the North for his trial and attending the execution of both martyrs having heard Blessed Thomas declare at his trial that he was willing to die for receiving priests into his home and, referring to Blessed Robert, said 'I received him as the messenger and the servant of God for my soul's sake.'

BLESSED GEORGE BEESLEY

Born at Goosnargh, Preston, Lancashire, circa 1563
Hanged, drawn and quartered at Fleet Street, London, on 1 July 1591
Beatified by Pope St John Paul II on 22 November 1987

RDAINED A PRIEST on 14 March 1587, Blessed George returned to England the following year on All Souls Day. At first he went to London where records reveal that he had clandestinely officiated at the wedding of a Catholic prisoner in the Marshalsea prison. He then went north, working on the mission in the area around Lancaster, Durham and York under the *alias* of Passelaw. That he was able to begin serving the Faithful at all, yet alone succeed in doing so for two years, was a great grace considering that, thanks to a spy in Paris, Sir Francis Walsingham had been informed that he was returning to England.

By summer 1590, Blessed George was moving near to London when he was arrested at the house of John and Margaret Gage at Haling in Surrey and brought to the Tower where he had to endure the particular attentions of Topcliffe who was at pains to extract as much information out of him through torture as possible, rendering

Blessed George almost unrecognisable to his friends. Having endured incarceration in the most cramped and cruel cell of 'Little Ease', he was moved to the Martin Tower where he scratched an inscription into the wall that is still visible today.

When Topcliffe had finished his work, Blessed George was transferred to Newgate prison for trial along with Blessed Montford Scott, and with him died.

BLESSED MONTFORD SCOTT

Born in Hawstead, Suffolk, circa 1550
Hanged, drawn and quartered at Fleet Street, London, on 1 July 1591
Beatified by Pope St John Paul II on 22 November 1987

ORN INTO A wealthy East Anglian family, Montford (or Monford) Scott was already an ardent Catholic as a young man, leaving Trinity Hall, Cambridge, without graduating because of this and, in his early twenties, he was included in a list of recusants. By 1574 he was studying at Douai but his studies were interrupted in December 1576 when he accompanied a priest on his way to Essex. They were quickly apprehended, being described by the Privy Council as 'wandering from place to place within this realm' in order to 'maliciously seduce Her Majesty's people from the truth and doctrine of the Gospel'. After a short spell in prison Blessed Montford returned to Douai and was ordained a priest in June 1577.

Within two months Scott was back in England and commencing fourteen years of active ministry, a ministry well attested to by government records. In 1578 he was arrested in Cambridge being sent to London 'with books, letters, writings and other trash' that he was found to possess. Released on bail, he alluded the authorities. Over the next five years spies reported sightings of him in Kent and in London. In 1584 searches for him were ordered in the north of England and, in Norwich, he was charged with 'distributing divers hallowed beads' and 'saying of divers Masses', but this was done in his absence. Likewise, the following year, he was cited before the Queen's Bench in London and declared an outlaw, this being done without anyone knowing where he was.

Five years were to pass before Topcliffe was to catch up with him when Blessed Montford was arrested in December 1590 at a house in his native Hawstead and dispatched for trial to London. Imprisoned at the King's Bench prison, he reconciled a fellow prisoner to the Catholic Church before attempting to bribe his way to freedom. But such a prize was this notably ascetic and infuriatingly allusive priest for Topcliffe, Blessed Montford stood little chance of escape and he was brought to trial at the same time as Blessed George Beesley and ultimately martyred with him.

BLESSED ROGER DICKENSON

Born in Lincolnshire
Hanged, drawn and quartered at Winchester on 7 July 1591
Beatified by Pope Pius XI on 15 December 1929

BLESSED ROGER DICKENSON was ordained a priest at Laon in 1583, one year after he entered the English College at Rheims. He was almost immediately dispatched to work on the mission in England which he pursued under a number of aliases such as Richard Johnson, Kinson, Lacey and Welby. Despite this he was arrested by the end of 1583 and examined on three occasions but never brought to trial. It is possible that he was exiled in 1585 but if that was so he was not away for long as he was soon working in and around Winchester, assisting the poor and visiting the prison. During one of these prison visits he first encountered Blessed Ralph Milner, a farm labourer with a large family who had become a Catholic, being arrested on the very day of his First Holy Communion. Not only did Blessed Ralph help Dickenson in his ministry amongst the prisoners but, and this was to cost him his life, he also gave him a place to stay.

In January 1591 they were both arrested and taken to the Clink in Southwark. After examination they were sent back to Winchester for trial. At the trial they were joined ass defendants by eight or nine Catholic women who were accused of permitting Blessed Roger to say Mass in their homes. All were condemned to death but, ultimately, the women were reprieved.

SAINT EDMUND GENNINGS

Born in Lichfield, Staffordshire, in 1566
Hanged, drawn and quartered at Gray's Inn, London, on 10 December 1591
Beatified by Pope Pius XI on 15 December 1929
Canonized by Pope St Paul VI on 25 October 1970

UCH OF OUR knowledge about St Edmund comes from a book, entitled *The life and death of Mr Edmund Geninges priest crowned with martyrdome at London, the 10 day of November in the year*

MD.XCI, written by the martyr's brother, John, who
became a Catholic after witnessing St Edmund's martyrdom, and subsequently becoming a Franciscan friar. His
brother relates that as a child, brought up as a Protestant,
the young saint was 'of modest behaviour ... little given to
play, much delighted to view the heaven and stars' and
gifted with visions in the night sky.

From a young age he came under the influence of his
Catholic schoolmaster and was introduced to Richard
Sherwood, a gentleman who took St Edmund on as his
page, effectively acting as a secret courier between him
and a Catholic prisoner in Lancaster. Both Sherwood and
St Edmund determined to make their way to Rheims to
train to become priests, the seventeen year old St Edmund
being sent on first.

As with not a few students at Douai College, ill health
was a severe problem for St Edmund and, seeming to be
suffering from consumption, he was sent home for the
good of his health. Getting as far as Le Harve and deeply
disappointed in his lot but firmly hopeful and trusting in
the power of prayer, he prayed for a cure, his prayers being
answered the night before he was due to sail to England,
and so he returned to his college. On 18 March 1590, with
a papal dispensation as he was only twenty-three and
therefore under the canonical age for ordination, he was
ordained a priest at Soissons.

In an age when all travel was somewhat hazardous, St
Edmund's journey to England, accompanied by brother
priests Blessed Alexander Rawlins and Sewell, was particularly difficult. They were robbed and briefly imprisoned
by Huguenots, shot at by pirates and caught in a storm
before finally reaching land at night under a cliff at
Whitby, Yorkshire. They were not, or ever going to be safe,
as within hours of landing a suspicious officer questioned

them as they rested at an inn but they were able to convince him that they were travellers from Newcastle who, having been caught in the storm, had been driven off course. St Edmund's journey did not improve: making his way back to his home city of Lichfield he discovered that since he had left England both his parents had died and his only living close relative was his brother, John. For six months St Edmund ministered in Lichfield before setting out to London where he knew that his brother had gone, though not his exact address. After some months he twice encountered him in the street but, John knowing that his brother was a priest, he refused to acknowledge him.

On All Souls' Day 1591, St Edmund was captured in a raid, led by Richard Topcliffe, along with St Polydore Plasden at the house of St Swithun Wells in Holborn. There was a struggle as an attempt was made to defend the priests at least until the Mass was finished and in the fracas Topcliffe was thrown down the stairs, cutting his head. St Edmund, still wearing his vestments, and the congregation were all taken to Newgate. Attempting to free his wife, St Swithun Wells was arrested the following day. All were tried at Westminster Hall on 4 December, St Edmund being presented for especial ridicule by being made to wear a jester's costume which had been found at St Swithun's house. As he was so young it was thought that the certainty of a horrendous death would be enough to persuade him to recant his faith but Topcliffe was left in no doubt that was not the case, taking his revenge on the saint first by having him cast into 'Little Ease', the cell where a prisoner could neither sit, stand or lie down, for the final days and nights of his earthly life. Vengeance continued at the scaffold when, again, the saint proved more than a match in strength of purpose to his tormentor. John Gennings, relying on eyewitness accounts of his

brother's execution, relates how St Edmund responded to
Topcliffe's cry 'Geninges, Geninges, confesse thy fault, thy
Popish treason, and the Queene by submission (no doubt)
will grant thee pardon', by mildly responding

> If to returne into England Priest, or to say Masse be
> Popish treason, I heere confesse I am a traytour; but
> I thinke not so. And therefore I acknowledge my
> selfe guilty of these thinges, not with repentance or
> sorrow of hart, but with an open protestation of
> inward ioy, that I have done so good deedes, which
> if they were to do agayne, I would by the permission
> and assistance of Almighty God accomplish the
> same, although with the hazard of a thousand lives.

> Which wordes M. Topliffe hearing, being much
> troubled therwith, scarce giving him leave to say a
> Pater noster, bad the Hangman turne the ladder,
> which in an instant being done, presently he caused
> him to be cut downe, the Blessed martyr in the
> sight of all the beholders, being yet able to stand
> on his feete, & casting his eyes towardes heaven,
> his senses were very little astonished, in so much
> that the Hangman was forced to trippe up his
> heeles from under him to make him fall on the
> blocke. And being dismembred, through very
> payne, in the hearing of many, with a lowde voyce
> he uttered these wordes, 'Oh it smartes', which M.
> Welles hearing, replyed thus: 'Alas sweete soule
> thy payne is great indeed, but almost past, pray for
> me now most holy Saynt, that mine may come.' He
> being ripped up, & his bowelles cast into the fire,
> if credit may be given to hundreds of People
> standing by, and to the Hangman himselfe, the
> blessed Martyr uttered (his hart being in the
> executioners   hand)   these   words,   Sancte
> Gregori ora pro me, which the Hangman hearing,
> with open mouth swore this damnable oath, 'Gods

woundes, See his hart is in my hand, and yet
Gregory in his mouth, o egregious Papist!' Thus
the afflicted Martyr even to the last of his torments
cryed for the ayde & succour of Saynts, and especially of S. Gregory his devoted patron, and our
countries Apostle that by his intercession he might
passe the sharpnes of that torment.

SAINT EUSTACE WHITE

Born in Louth, Lincolnshire, in 1559
Hanged, drawn and quartered at Tyburn, London,
10 December 1591
Beatified by Pope Pius XI on 15 December 1929
Canonized by Pope St Paul VI on 25 October 1970

T EUSTACE'S FATHER was a prominent citizen of
Louth and held the office of Warden of the town
corporation on four occasions. A staunch Protestant, he cursed his son on his conversion to Catholicism.
From 31 October 1584, St Eustace studied at Rheims for
two years before being sent on to the English College in
Rome. On 16 April 1588 he was ordained a deacon but the
date of his priestly ordination has not been discovered,
though he certainly was ordained by the autumn as he is
known to have been a priest as he passed through Rheims
on his way back to England.

Although he was noticed by a government spy in Paris
as he made his return journey, St Eustace managed to
allude capture until September 1591 when he was apprehended in Dorset thanks to having engaged a lawyer in
conversation after a chance encounter, the lawyer suggesting that they pause for refreshments at an inn in Blandford,

his real intention being to alert the authorities of his suspicions that St Eustace was a priest. St Eustace had actually left the inn and was not present when officers came to arrest him but he returned to recover his breviary which he had accidentally left there.

After a public disputation with local ministers in which the saint was effortlessly convincing regarding the Catholic cause, eliciting the praise and sympathy of the townsfolk, he was taken to the Bridewell prison in London where he was chained, starved and then tortured by Topcliffe. St Eustace wrote to Fr Henry Garnet about his ordeal:

> The morrow after Simon and Jude's day I was hanged at the wall from the ground, my manacles fast locked into a staple as high as I could reach upon a stool: the stool taken away where I hanged from a little after 8 o'clock in the morning until after 4 in the afternoon, without any ease or comfort at all, saving that Topcliffe came in and told me that the Spaniards were come into Southwark by our means: 'For lo, do you not hear the drums' (for then the drums played in honour of the Lord Mayor). The next day after also I was hanged up an hour or two: such is the malicious minds of our adversaries.

At his trial in Westminster Hall during the first days of December, St Eustace was joined by a fellow student from his Roman years, St Ploydore Plasden. The two were also executed together along with three laymen, St Eustace praying for his oppressors until the end and declaring,

> If I had never so many lives, I would think them very few to bestow upon your Tyburns to defend my religion. I wish I had a great many more than one, you should have them all one after another.

SAINT PLOYDORE PLASDEN

Born in London in 1563
Hanged, drawn and quartered at Tyburn, London,
10 December 1591
Beatified by Pope Pius XI on 15 December 1929
Canonized by Pope St Paul VI on 25 October 1970

ORN THE SON of a horner (a man who worked in horn) near the bridge over the River Fleet, Oliver Palmer (for that was this saint's baptismal name) entered Douai College at Rheims before being sent on to the English College in Rome, arriving there in April 1586 and assuming the alias of Polydore Plasden. Later that same year, on 7 December, he was ordained a priest and remained in Rome until March 1588 when he set out for Rheims and then, five months later, for England.

For over three years St Polydore managed to minister in London without being caught until he was arrested along with St Edmund Gennings at the house of St Swithun Wells in one of Topcliffe's successful raids. Along with others, the two priests were tried together, St Polydore stating to the court,

> They find us guilty of treason for exercising our priestly function, which was in all ages an honourable calling, as you the learned on the Bench have read in your own laws and histories, if you dare to speak the truth.

Among the spectators at Tyburn for his execution was Sir Walter Raleigh. Hearing St Polydore pray for the queen and the whole realm he intervened, proposing that a royal pardon should be sought. Topcliffe remained unmoved asking the priest,

If the King of Spain or the Pope would come into
this country by force for no other end precisely,
but by his canonical law to establish that thou
believest and which thou thinkest to be the true
Catholic faith as you call it, tell me, wouldst thou
resist them?

To which the martyr replied,

I am a Catholic priest. Therefore I would never
fight or counsel others to fight against my religion,
for that were to deny my faith. O Christ, I will never
deny Thee for a thousand lives.

And so the execution proceeded, except that, due to the
insistence of Raleigh, the victim was allowed to die by
hanging and only then was his body mutilated according
to the letter of the law.

1592

BLESSED WILLIAM PATENSON

Born in Durham, date of birth unknown
Hanged, drawn and quartered at Tyburn, London, 22
January 1592
Beatified by Pope Pius XI on 15 December 1929

Blessed William was admitted to the English College at Rheims on 1 May 1584 and ordained a priest in September 1587. He may have remained at the college for up to fifteen months after ordination before setting out to England to minister in the West Country. Just before Christmas 1591 he was arrested while saying Mass in a house in Clerkenwell, London. Quickly brought to trial and condemned, he spent his final days ministering to his fellow prisoners and, according to one account, converted six condemned men the night before he died.

BLESSED THOMAS PORMORT

Born at Little Limber, Lincolnshire, circa 1560
Hanged, drawn and quartered in St Paul's Churchyard,
London, on 20 February 1592
Beatified by Pope St John Paul II on 22 November
1987.

ODSON OF THE Anglican Archbishop of Canterbury, John Whitgift, then an up-and-coming Protestant cleric in Grimsby, Blessed Thomas was
educated at Trinity College, Cambridge, where Whitgift
had become Master as well as holding the university
position of Regius Professor of Divinity. Pormort did not
graduate from the university, presumably because he had
become a Catholic by this time. He began his priestly
formation at Rheims on 15 January 1581 but was sent on
to the English College, Rome, in May of the same year, being
ordained a priest at the Lateran Basilica on 26 August 1587.

Rather than heading north to England, Blessed Thomas
became a member of the household of Owen Lewis,
Bishop of Cassano in the Kingdom of Naples, one of those
who had been instrumental in establishing the English
colleges at Douai and in Rome and who had served as a
vicar general for St Charles Borromeo in Milan. Lewis sent
Blessed Thomas up to Milan where he became Prefect of
Studies at the Swiss College but he did not remain long
for, in the words of Henry Garnet, 'he began to see the
vanities of this world and to despise its snares, and
resolved to return home, where, for Christ's sake (if He so
willed) he would spend his life.'

Disguised as a servant, and using a name well known
to him as his alias—Whitgift—Blessed Thomas arrived

back in England where he sought and was assisted by St Robert Southwell in finding lodgings in London. His ministry was brief. He was first apprehended, thanks to being seen by an apostate priest, in July 1591but he seems to have escaped only to be caught again two months later after reconciling a haberdasher, John Barwys, who lived by St Paul's Cathedral. Blessed Thomas was taken to Bridewell prison and then to Topcliffe's home where he was brutally tortured in Topcliffe's illegally set up torture chamber. Having been racked a number of times, some of the martyr's internal organs possibly having been rup-tured, Blessed Thomas needed a truss to support the rupture when he was brought to trial.

While Blessed Thomas held his counsel during torture, Topcliffe was reckless in his slander of the queen and Archbishop Whitgift and, after Pormort's return to prison, the priest was able to smuggle out notes of what Topcliffe had said to others, this news quickly finding its way to the Privy Council and being referred to at Pormort's trial on 8 February 1592. Topcliffe, who hated the Archbishop of Canterbury, had attempted to cajole Blessed Thomas into saying that he was Archbishop Whitgift's bastard child and telling Blessed Thomas of sexual fantasies with regard to the queen and Topcliffe himself.

After being sentenced, the Archbishop attempted to intervene, asking that his chaplains should be allowed to 'reason' with Pormort. A vengeful Topcliffe reacted by obtaining the Council's order for execution to proceed and, on the freezing cold morning of 20 February, outside the house of the man he had converted, Topcliffe pro-longed the martyr's suffering by making the almost disa-bled Blessed Thomas stand in just his shirt on the steps of the gallows while he attempted to bully him into retracting the report of his dangerously foolhardy slander against the queen and archbishop. This Blessed Thomas would not do and, to the accompaniment of the taunts of a terrorised John Barwys who had been offered his life if he renounced the Catholic faith, the martyr died.

BLESSED JOSEPH LAMBTON

Born in Malton, Yorkshire, in 1568
Hanged, drawn and quartered at Newcastle on 24 July 1592
Beatified by Pope St John Paul II on 22 November 1987

THE YOUNGEST PRIEST of the Douai martyrs to die, Blessed Joseph Lambton was born into a locally renowned family, his uncle going on to be the second Archpriest of England. Joseph entered the English College at Rheims in 1584. He was sent to the English College in Rome five years later and ordained at the Lateran on 28 March 1592 having been granted a dispensation for being two months under the age canonically required. Setting out for England in late spring and hoping to minister in Westmorland, he was arrested by a vigilant town clerk in Newcastle upon Tyne soon after setting foot ashore. Blessed Joseph's travelling companion, Blessed Edward Waterson, was also arrested in the town while he was attempting to procure a passport to permit him to travel by sea to London.

Both priests were tried and condemned to death on 20 July 1592. The night before his execution, Blessed Joseph cheerfully remarked to Waterson that they should be merry for 'tomorrow I hope that we shall have a heavenly breakfast'. The judicial execution was one of the worst hatchet jobs meted out by a hangman to one of the English martyrs. The executioner was a criminal who had saved his own life by taking on his bloody office. He was also woefully inexperienced and, halfway through the dismembering of the martyr he fled in panic, the butchery to be completed by a French surgeon who was duly paid twenty shillings for his troubles. Hoping to terrorize Blessed Edward Waterson into recanting his faith, the sheriff brought one of Blessed Joseph's quarters to Waterson who, rather than reacting as hoped, reverently kissed the holy relic that was put before him.

1593

BLESSED EDWARD WATERSON

Born in London, date of birth unknown
Hanged, drawn and quartered at Newcastle upon
Tyne, 7 January 1593
Beatified by Pope Pius XI on 15 December 1929

S A YOUNG man Blessed Edward was a traveller, journeying to Turkey where, it is said, he was offered the hand in marriage of the daughter of a wealthy Turk, provided that he converted to Islam. This he did not do but on his way back to England, stopping in Rome, he found himself convinced and moved by Dr Richard Smith at the English College. Becoming a Catholic in 1558, he proceeded to the English College at Rheims, being ordained a priest four years later. Once back in England his ministry lasted but a few months before his arrest and condemnation in Newcastle upon Tyne. According to Challoner, who was in possession of letters written by a contemporary to Douai, the horses that were to drag the martyr's hurdle to the scaffold refused to move, Blessed Edward having to be conveyed to his execution on foot.

Blessed James Bird

Born in Winchester circa 1574
Hanged, drawn and quartered at Winchester on 25
March 1593
Beatified by Pope Pius XI on 15 December 1929

A S A YOUNG man, Blessed James became a Catholic, venturing over to Douai College in Rheims in the hope that he might be called to the priesthood. This was not to be but he returned to Winchester as a noticeably zealous and devout man. This came to the attention of the authorities and he was arrested, charged with having converted to Catholicism and, therefore, believing in the religious supremacy of the pope. This was high treason and although he knew well what the penalty for this was, he refused to recant his faith by attending Church of England services. After some time in prison the nineteen year old was martyred by being hanged, drawn and quartered on Lady Day, suffering, it was said, courageously and cheerfully.

Blessed Antony Page

Born in Harrow-on-the-Hill, Middlesex, circa 1563
Hanged, drawn and quartered at York on 20 April
1593
Beatified by Pope St John Paul II on 22 November
1987

F A GENTRY family, Blessed Antony was educated at Christchurch College, Oxford. He was received at the English College, Rheims, on 30 September 1584 being ordained a priest at Soissons on 21 September 1591, setting out for England the following January. For just over a year he was to minister to the Catholics of Yorkshire, even in that time catching the attention of a government spy.

As the Christmas festivities drew to an end, on 2 February 1593 the Earl of Huntingdon, President of the Council of the North, ordered an intense crackdown against Catholics and priests in particular. Blessed Antony was discovered and arrested at Heworth Hall, then just outside the city of York, the pursuivants discovering him hiding under a haystack in an outhouse. Both Blessed Antony and the owner of the house, William Thwing, were brought to trial and both could have been executed but Thwing's life was saved by his sister, Anne, stepping forward to state that it was her, not her brother, who was responsible for harbouring the priest. For this, Anne Thwing may have spent the rest of her life in prison. Cheerfully, Blessed Antony Page awaited his martyrdom, writing many letters to possible converts and one to his mother, saying that he was offering his life to God for her conversion.

BLESSED WILLIAM DAVIES

Born in Croes-yn-eirias, Denbighshire, circa 1558
Hanged, drawn and quartered at Beaumaris Castle,
Anglesey, on 27 July 1593
Beatified by Pope St John Paul II on 22 November
1987

HE GRANDSON OF the most renowned harpist of his day, William Davies may have been educated at St Edmund Hall, Oxford, before being admitted to the English College at Rheims in 1582. After priestly ordination on 5 April 1585 he returned to north Wales, ministering in the area around Plas Penrhyn and finding lodgings in the home of Robert Pugh. But when, in 1586, the Earl of Pembroke, President of the Council of Wales, vigorously renewed persecution of Catholics, Blessed William and his friends had to flee to the hills, finding refuge in a cave in the Rhiwledyn cliffs where they enterprisingly set up a small printing press. It was there that the first known book to be printed in Wales was printed, the anonymously authored *Y drych Cristianogawl—The Christian Mirror.* The cave was raided in April 1587 but Blessed William and his companions escaped.

In March 1592 he and Robert Pugh were less fortunate, Blessed William being arrested along with four young men whom they were attempting to smuggle out of the country so that they could start formation at the English College in Valladolid, Spain. Pugh again escaped—Blessed William was taken to Beaumaris Castle where he was held in solitary confinement for a month before being allowed to receive visitors, becoming a magnate for brave Catholics who sought his blessing and to whom they could make their confessions.

In July 1592 Blessed William and the four hopeful seminarians were tried and all were found guilty—the priest for being a priest, the four young men being granted the mercy of the judge declaring that their crime was not attending church, not the capital crime of assisting a priest. Strenuous attempts were made to convince Blessed William to recant his faith as he was moved from one prison to another. This having failed he was brought to trial for a second time at Beaumaris, this time being given the death sentence. Throughout his trials and imprisonment the great support and affection of the local population was very clear to the authorities and when it came to arranging his execution they were constrained to employ a hangman, and even to obtain the materials required for the execution, from Chester, forty-two miles away from Beaumaris. Speaking from the scaffold, Blessed William declared that

> the cause for which he died was no other than his priestly character, [and he] prayed that his innocent blood, which he joyfully shed for his religion, might not cry to heaven for vengeance, but rather plead for mercy for that island, that it might once more be illustrated with the light of faith which it had lost.

Of the four men arrested with the martyr in 1592, two went on to be ordained priests.

1594

Blessed William Harrington

Born in Felixkirk, North Riding of Yorkshire, in 1566
Hanged, drawn and quartered at Tyburn, London,
on 18 February 1594
Beatified by Pope Pius XI on 15 December 1929

T THE AGE of fifteen, Blessed William Harrington met St Edmund Campion at his family home of Mount St John, Felixkirk, the meeting inspiring the young man to become a priest, entering the college at Rheims in September 1582, only to leave in 1584 to try his vocation as a Jesuit at the order's college in Tournai. Poor health was to prevent him joining the religious congregation and cause him to return to England where he was quickly betrayed by a man who had been a tailor in Rheims who recognized Blessed William. Probably because of his youth—he was just eighteen at the time—he was not punished severely but rather returned to his parent's home.

Seven years later, Blessed William set sail once more for Rheims, this time being ordained a priest in March 1592 by the papal nuncio, Cardinal Filippo Sega, before

returning to England in the summer. One year was granted
to him to minister in the West Country before his capture
at the house of Henry Donne, brother of the poet, John.
Henry Donne was imprisoned for harbouring him, dying
in prison from fever. Blessed William was thrown into
Bridewell prison and then transferred to Newgate where
he was interrogated and racked before trial and condemnation for being a Catholic priest. It was to be some
months before he was martyred, possibly because it was
hoped that he would recant his faith. But when the day
came and his body was cut down after hanging it is
recorded that 'he struggled with the hangman' as the latter
was about to disembowel him, a natural involuntary
reaction, but one that gives piquancy to a verse of the
hymn, 'Who are these like stars appearing':

> These are they who have contended
> for their Saviour's honour long,
> wrestling on till life was ended,
> following not the sinful throng;
> these who well the fight sustained,
> triumph through the Lamb have gained.

BLESSED JOHN CORNELIUS

Born in Bodmin, Cornwall, in 1554.
Hanged, drawn and quartered at Dorchester on 16
March 1594
Beatified by Pope Pius XI on 15 December 1929

T IS PROBABLY because Blessed John was born into a poor Irish family on the estate of Sir John Arundell that he was well educated and able to secure a place at Exeter College, Oxford, becoming a Fellow there in 1575. Despite being a well-known centre for illegal Catholic activities, Cornelius was expelled from the college on 3 August 1578 for being a Catholic. He travelled to Rheims where he entered Douai College before continuing his studies in Rome, where he was ordained a priest, probably in 1582. He must have been a gifted preacher as he was chosen to preach before the pope (Gregory XIII) on St Stephen's Day in the Sistine Chapel, an English College privilege up until 1870. A contemporary, Fr John Gerard, wrote that Blessed John was 'so famous in preaching that all Catholics followed him as children do their nurses when they long for milk.'

In September 1583 Blessed John left Rome for England, working as a chaplain for the Arundell family and those living on their estate, becoming renowned for his 'sweet and plausible tongue'. He ministered in London as well, as Sir John Arundell resided there for some years, and he became known as an effective exorcist. When Sir John died in 1590 Blessed John accompanied his widow to Chideock Castle in Dorset where he worked until his betrayal by one of the servants in 1594. Two other servants were arrested with him—Blessed John Carey and Blessed Patrick

Salmon, both from Dublin—along with another layman, Blessed Thomas Bosgrove, who was a nephew of Sir John, arrested, it seems, for merely offering a hat to the priest as he was being led away.

First interrogated locally by, among others, Sir Walter Raleigh, Blessed John was sent to London in the hope that information might be extracted from him through racking. This having failed, he was sent back to Dorset for trial and execution, along with the three who were caught with him. While in prison, Blessed John sought admission to the Society of Jesus, an aspiration that he had entertained while in Rome but was then denied to him. Fr Henry Garnet, while doing his best to encourage the priest, said that he did not have the authority to admit him to the Society. However, on his own initiative, Blessed John made the Jesuit vows before three witnesses, asking them to inform Garnet of what he had done.

On the day of execution Blessed John was the last to die, all four men were offered the possibility of pardon if they renounced their faith—all refused. As he came to the gallows Blessed John kissed them, uttering, 'O good Cross, long desired!'. The deaths were witnessed by Raleigh who denied Blessed John the opportunity of addressing the crowd, but the martyr had made known once again his steadfast faith when signing a final letter from prison with the words, 'Yours, John, one about to die for a moment that he may live for ever.'

SAINT JOHN BOSTE

Born at Dufton, Westmorland, circa 1543
Hanged, drawn and quartered at Durham on 24 July
1594
Beatified by Pope Pius XI on 15 December 1929
Canonized by Pope St Paul VI on 25 October 1970

ORN AT WELLYNG Manor, Dufton, and educated at Queen's College, Oxford, where he became a Fellow in 1572, the future saint began his working life as a teacher at Appleby grammar school and as a Protestant minister. In 1576 he became a Catholic and was immediately expelled from his fellowship for 'forsaking his ministry' and 'contradicting sound Christian doctrine'. On 4 August 1580 St John entered the English College at Rheims along with a young man, Gerard Clibborn, whom he had been tutoring, being ordained a priest on 4 March 1581 at Châlons-sur-Marne. Within weeks he was sent to England, landing at Hartlepool, from where he began his ministry in the northern counties and Scotland and becoming one of the pursuivants' most wanted priests in the north. St John eluded the authorities until his betrayal by a renegade Catholic in a house near Brancepeth in Co. Durham on 10 September 1593.

After his arrest he was transported to Windsor where he was examined by Topcliffe and cruelly wracked a number of times, rendering him barely able to walk. Having been taken back to Durham St John was tried together with the priest, Blessed John Ingram, and a Catholic layman, Blessed George Swallowell, all being condemned to death. During the trial Swallowell, a former Protestant minister, began to waiver in his Catholic convictions but, upon encouragement from St John, he remained steadfast, asking the saint for forgiveness. St John responded by giving him absolution before the whole court. Blessed Christopher Robinson witnessed St John's sacrifice, reporting that as he mounted the scaffold, the condemned man prayed the Angelus.

BLESSED JOHN INGRAM

Born at Stoke Edith, Herefordshire, in 1565
Hanged, drawn and quartered at Gateshead on 26 July 1594
Beatified by Pope Pius XI on 15 December 1929

EING CAPTURED BY Calvinist soldiers on his way from Douai to Rheims must have given the future martyr a very keen sense of what lay ahead of him when, after further studies at the English College in Rome and ordination there at the Lateran in 1589, he returned to his homeland in 1591. Spies had served the government well as Blessed John's return was expected, but the authorities did not bargain for his landing in Scotland where he served for eighteen months as chaplain to Sir Walter Lindsay of Balgavies Castle, near Forfar.

Ingram was, however, a marked man and when he did finally cross the border he was immediately arrested and taken to Berwick before being brought to the Tower of London for torture, but the officers were unable to extract any information from him. Whilst in prison he wrote letters and scratched onto his cell walls epigrams and verses in Latin. The latter have not survived but some of his letters have. In one letter he prays that he might have 'constancy, courage, and zeal in my holy enterprise, for the spirit is ready, but the flesh is weak.' In another letter he wrote, 'And although in my native country I have taken great pains in God's vineyard, yet I doubt not, if God will strengthen me ... [that] I shall purchase for our Babylonic soil more favour by my death.'

Having been sent back to Durham, St John Boste and the beati John Ingram and George Swallowell were tried and condemned together, Blessed John giving his life for the Faith at Gateshead on 26 July 1594. Newcastle's accounts records the price of the proceedings:

> Paide for charges att the execution of the semynarie priete in Gateside John Ingram—2 shillings and 6 pence. Paide for hinginge his quarters of the gibbettes: 18 pence and for panyer which brought his quarters to towne 4 pence—22 pence. Paide for a locke for towlboothe dore in Gateside—3 shillings 4 pence.

BLESSED EDWARD OSBALDESTON

Born in Lancashire circa 1560
Hanged, drawn and quartered at York on 16 November 1594
Beatified by Pope St John Paul II on 22 November 1987

LESSED EDWARD WAS ordained priest on 21 September 1585, having studied at the English College in Rheims for some years before. Unusually, he continued to live in Rheims until 29 April 1589 when he set out for England. For five years he ministered in Yorkshire, occasionally attracting the attention of government spies but evading arrest until 30 September 1594 when he was seized at an inn in Tollerton, near York. His capture came about through the bad luck of Thomas

Clarke, a former priest turned spy, recognizing him at the inn. Being tried in York, the martyr was executed alongside several common criminals.

1595

SAINT ROBERT SOUTHWELL

Born at Horsham St Faith, Norfolk, in 1561
Hanged, drawn and quartered at Tyburn, London, on 21
February 1595
Beatified by Pope Pius XI on 15 December 1929
Canonized by Pope St Paul VI on 25 October 1970

Born into a gentry family whose home had been built in and around the refectory of a suppressed priory, the young St Robert was teased by his father with the title 'Father Robert'—he must have been a pious child. At the age of fifteen he and one of his cousins arrived at Douai College, being sent from there to the Jesuit school, Anchin College, but boarding at the English College. In 1578 he travelled to Rome with the intention of becoming a Jesuit, a hope that was at first denied him but, upon his appealing, he was admitted to the novitiate house of Sant'Andrea in Rome on 17 October 1578.

Having completed his novitiate, St Robert entered the English College, Rome, studying philosophy and theology at the Roman College but also acting as a secretary to the rector and, ultimately, being made Prefect of Studies. But all of this was not what he desired most, as he wrote to the General of the Society of Jesus: 'in the same way as Your Paternity approves of my present work among the English, so by the inspiration of God may you also approve of my service in England itself, with the highest hope of martyrdom'.

With Henry Garnet, St Robert rode out of Rome on 8 May 1586, the two making their way via Douai to Folkestone and then travelling separately, St Robert heading to London, the principal ground for his ministry. Letters from him to Rome survive as does a significant collection of poetry for which he would have been remembered even if he had not led such a heroic life.

From the beginning, the mission was dangerous, St Robert writing that the pursuivants prowled 'lynx-eyed' and that he was 'Hemmed in by daily perils, never safe for even a brief moment'. 'Such is the multitude of spies,' he wrote, 'that we cannot set foot out of doors, nor walk in the streets, without danger to our lives.' St Robert's letters reveal that he narrowly alluded capture a number of times and, in 1586, he warned future missioners to 'gird themselves for heavier trials than their companions have hitherto suffered, for the sea is more boisterous than usual and swept by fiercer storms.'

Such storms were to become evermore rapacious in the wake of the failed Spanish Armada, St Robert writing, 'Our rulers turned their arms from foreign foes against their own sons and with inhuman ferocity vented the hatred they had conceived against the Spaniards on their fellow citizens.' In the late summer of 1588 seventeen priests, nine layman and one woman were executed within just three months on the grounds of religious treason.

St Robert's life became a little more settled under the protection of Anne Howard, countess of Arundel and Surrey, in whose Spitalfields house he was able to set up a printing press: 'The work of God,' wrote St Robert, 'is being pressed forward, often enough by delicate women who have taken on the courage of men.' During this time he corresponded with Anne's husband, St Philip Howard, who was imprisoned in the Tower, these letters forming the substance of St Robert's longest prose work, *An epistle of comfort, to the reverend priestes, and to the honorable, worshipful, and other of the laye sort, restrayned in durance for the Catholicke faith.* The published work advertised that it had been printed in Paris, a ruse concealing its true place of printing in Anne Howard's house. In the book St Robert, citing Scripture and the Fathers of the Church, sought to encourage those who were suffering for the Catholic Faith, especially those awaiting execution. In the final pages of the work he writes,

> And we have God be thanked such martyrquellers now in authoritye, as meane if they may have theyre will, to make Saynctes enough to furnishe all our Churches with treasure when it shall please God to restore them to theyre true honoures.

Other works were also published including *A Shorte Rule of Good Life, Funeral Teares* and, his only political tract, *An Humble Supplication to her Majestie, written in response to the proclamation A declaration of great troubles pretended against the realme by a number of seminarie priests and Jesuists.* The publication of the latter work resulted in the persecution of Catholics being pursued with even greater diligence and St Robert had to be sent from London in an attempt to preserve him from capture, his distinctive auburn hair making him easier to be identified than most.

It was returning to London that Topcliffe discovered St Robert's whereabouts, thanks to information extracted from Anne Bellamy, in whose brother's house near Harrow the saint was hoping to find rest for the night of 26 June 1592. Anne herself was a prisoner in the Gatehouse yet she had fallen pregnant, possibly having been raped, and was undoubtedly horrendously scared of her evil captor. St Robert was immediately taken to Topcliffe's house and his infamous torture chamber before being transferred to the Gatehouse and then to the Tower. Southwell had been using his alias of Cotton and refused to reveal his real name but Topcliffe was certain of his prey and the saint was held in solitary confinement at the Tower for two and a half years until being taken to Newgate and then to his trial on 20 February 1595. During this time he endured Topcliffe's most recent vicious torture, the 'wall torture' where the victim was hung by manacled wrists from a hook high up on a wall. Sir Robert Cecil, the queen's chief minister, on seeing the broken body of St Robert, remarked that he had thought that the wall torture was 'not possible for a man to bear. And yet I have seen Robert Southwell hanging by it still as a tree-trunk and no one able to drag one word from his mouth.'

The authorities hoped that by hanging a notorious highwayman with the martyr, the crowd's attention would be deflected from priestly poet. Instead, the ploy backfired in that the execution attracted a larger gathering than usual. Somehow St Robert managed to keep his head above the mud as he was dragged to Tyburn and was permitted to make a short speech before his death in which he quoted lines of St Paul, 'Whether we live, we live to the Lord, or whether we die, we die to the Lord; therefore, whether we live or die, we belong to the Lord.' Having prayed for queen and country and called upon the angels and saints to assist him, the cart on which he stood was drawn away. Henry Garnet witnessed the scene and saw that when the sergeant stepped forward to cut the rope so that the disembowelling could begin with the saint alive, Lord Mountjoy stepped forward and stopped him. As the crowds began to roar that the man should be allowed to die before being butchered, the sheriff then attempted to cut the rope, but frightened by the crowd's growing unrest he stopped leaving the hangman to pull on St Robert's legs until his body went limp. Taking down the body, the hangman then cradled it in his arms before beheading the saint and, probably without much conviction, holding up the severed head, declaring as was customary, 'Here is the head of a traitor.' No shout of 'Traitor!' echoed back, those present bearing their heads in respect instead.

After St Robert's death, Henry Garnet gathered together and published his poems, some words of his prose perhaps giving the meaning to both his life and death: 'Love is not ruled with reason, but with love. It neither regardeth what can nor what shall be done, but only what it itself desireth to do. No difficulty can stay it, no impossibility appal it.'

BLESSED ALEXANDER RAWLINS

Born in Oxford in 1560
Hanged, drawn and quartered at York on 7 April 1595
Beatified by Pope Pius XI on 15 December 1929

DUCATED AT WINCHESTER and Oxford, Blessed Alexander found employment in an apothecary in Denham, Buckinghamshire. By June 1586 he had become a Catholic, being arrested in that month along with St Swithun Wells and Fr Christopher Dryland, a seminary priest, and imprisoned in Newgate. Being

released he was soon incarcerated again and was held in
the Fleet prison at the end of the same year, awaiting
banishment for being a Catholic recusant. This exile
encouraged him to not only persist in the Catholic faith
but also to become a priest and, after travelling extensively
including a pilgrimage to Rome, he enrolled in Douai
College, then at Rheims, in December 1587.

On 18 March 1590 Blessed Alexander was ordained a
priest at Soissons, setting out for England the following
month. Back in England his missionary fields were Yorkshire and Durham, sometimes working under the alias of
Alexander Yeale, Yeale being his mother's maiden name.
No more is known about him until his arrest on Christmas
Day 1594 at the house of Blessed Thomas Warcop in
Winston, Durham, the Warcop family being taken into
custody as well. Letters from the beatus, along with his
will, are held at the English College, Rome. In them he
describes his prison as a 'castle of comfort and palace of
pleasure'. Being condemned to death, Blessed Alexander
was martyred along with St Henry Walpole, the two
sharing a hurdle on their last journey. An eyewitness
account records how Blessed Alexander, who was first to
die, kissed the gallows and rope, repeating the name of
Jesus until his last breath hanging from the gallows.

Saint Henry Walpole

Born at Dorking, Norfolk, in 1558
Hanged, drawn and quartered at York on 7 April 1595
Beatified by Pope Pius XI on 15 December 1929
Canonized by Pope St Paul VI on 25 October 1970

The second priest to die at York on 7 April was St Henry Walpole, an alumnus of Peterhouse College, Cambridge, and Gray's Inn, he was the eldest son of the ten children born to Christopher and Margery Walpole, the Walpoles having lived in Norfolk for over six hundred years and, in a future century, were to give Britain her first Prime Minister. It is not certain if the Walpole family had conformed to the Church of England but given that their eldest son did not receive his degree at Cambridge it is certain that by 1578, having been a member of Peterhouse for 3 years, St Henry had become a Catholic and therefore would not take the oath necessary for graduating.

Gray's Inn itself was a hotbed of Catholic activity and, with the cover of being a lawyer, St Henry attended the disputations in the Tower, the trial and execution of St Edmund Campion in 1581, some of the martyr's blood splashing onto him as his entrails were flung into the fire. The witness of the saint's life and death was a life-changing moment for St Henry. He wrote a poem as a tribute to Campion, a poem for which there was a great demand after it was printed. The publicity that his ode garnered incensed the government who strenuously attempted to discover who the author was and who printed it. In the second aim they were successful and condemned the printer to having his ears cut off. St Henry was suspected of being the author and decided to leave London, taking refuge in a hiding place at his family's home, Anmer Hall (country house of the Duke and Duchess of Cambridge from 2015) until it was safer to carefully make his way to the coast and the continent. To do this he journeyed north to Newcastle where he took a ship for France, ultimately arriving at the English College in Rheims on 7 July 1582. Ten months later he became a student at the English College, Rome, seeking admission to the Society of Jesus in 1584, completing his novitiate at Verdun and being ordained a priest in Paris on 17 December 1588. Three of St Henry's brothers and a cousin were to become Jesuit priests.

After some work in Italy, St Henry was sent to Flanders where he acted as chaplain to English men fighting in the Spanish army, a standard bearer in the regiment of Sir William Stanley being one Guy Fawkes. When the town of Flushing was captured by anti-Spanish troops, St Henry was arrested and put in prison where he remained until January 1590 when his brother, Michael, arrived from England with a ransom to procure his release. Being freed, St Henry spent two years working on the continent, work that included translating Persons' response to the queen's 1591 edict against seminary priests, a work that a government spy was able to send the Privy Council.

Two years were spent in Spain where St Henry was minister at the English College in Valladolid and then, after being presented to Philip II at the Escorial, he was sent to England, landing at Bridlington, Yorkshire, in the first days of December 1593: he and those whom he had travelled with were captured at Kilham by sunset of their first day in England, 7 December, and taken to York Castle. St Henry professed his priesthood but would reveal nothing more. He was sent to London and thrown into solitary confinement at the Tower, his first official examination with Topcliffe taking place on 27 April. He was racked many times, the torturers managing to wring names of students in seminaries out of him but not the name of anyone in England. Still, Topcliffe reckoned, the torture was slowly achieving its desired end and thus he continued to torture and terrorize the saint for a further nine months, at the beginning of which he could still write clearly, but not by the end. And what was the evidence of the state of his handwriting?—poems written by St Henry during his final days, seen by Frs Garnet and Gerard, that contemplated Our Lady and the angels, and Christ triumphant in His Passion.

Finally in the spring of 1595 St Henry was transferred to York for trial and martyrdom, being hung before he could finish his prayers.

BLESSED WILLIAM FREEMAN

Born in Manthorp Yorkshire, date of birth unknown
Hanged, drawn and quartered in Warwick on 13
August 1595
Beatified by Pope Pius XI on 15 December 1929

FTER OBTAINING HIS B.A. in 1580, Blessed William left Magdalen College, Oxford, to work in London. On 21 January 1586 he witnessed the martyrdom of Blessed Edward Stransham for his priesthood at Tyburn. This event made a deep impression on him and, if he was not already a Catholic by this date, he soon became one because by 4 May he had entered the English College at Rheims, being ordained a priest on 19 September 1587 and leaving for England in the first days of 1589: so far, a familiar story. But his journey, along with four other priests was not uneventful yet neither were the company ill-prepared. Apparently, the crew of the ship that was to take them up the Thames were found to be plotting to kill the priests. The priests, armed with rapiers, drew them and forced the sailors below deck.

Landing at Gravesend, Blessed William made for Warwickshire and Worcestershire, local Catholic tradition suggesting that he was in touch with several of William Shakespeare's friends. Working under the alias of Mason, for, as a friend put it to him, he was to be 'a workman and layer of stones in the building of God's church.', Blessed William ministered, evading capture several times, for six years until his arrest on 5 January 1595. He was caught hiding his breviary under his hat but with no other evidence that he was a priest and he had no intention of telling the pursuivants either, thus he escaped trial at the Lenten assizes but he was betrayed by another prisoner and was submitted to the assizes of 11 and 12 August: he is said to have started singing the *Te Deum* when his death sentence was handed down. He hoped to be the first of the condemned to die at his execution the next day but the sheriff set his hopes that horror of the deaths of others might frighten Blessed William into recanting his faith. The martyr assured the sheriff that even if he had many lives he would willingly give up them all for the sake of Him who had died to save him and, loudly praying Psalm 41, 'As the hart desires after the fountains of water, so does my soul after thee, O, my God. Oh, when shall I come and appear before thy face?', he prepared to enter eternal life.

1597

BLESSED CHRISTOPHER ROBINSON

Born at Woodside, Cumberland, circa 1567
Hanged, drawn and quartered at Carlisle on 5 April
1597
Beatified by Pope St John Paul II on 22 November 1987

LESSED CHRISTOPHER ROBINSON was ordained a priest by Cardinal Philip Sega in Rheims on 24 February 1592, having been a member of the English College at Rheims for almost three years. The date that he set out for the mission in England is also recorded—1 September 1592—the priest returning to his home area to minister. Two years later Blessed Christopher was present at the trial and martyrdom of St John Boste in Durham, writing an account of the proceedings in a letter to a friend afterwards.

Thanks to the work of Thomas Lancaster, a priest catcher in the pay of the Bishop of Carlisle, Blessed Christopher was arrested on 4 March 1597 in the home of Leonard and Margaret Musgrave, Johnby Hall, near Penrith. The Musgraves were to be granted a royal pardon but the priest was to be condemned to death. In prison a Protestant relative, Henry Robinson, then Provost of Queen's College, Oxford, but later to become Bishop of Carlisle, came to visit the condemned priest, hoping to coax him to renounce his faith with promises of pardon and support in the future, yet his efforts were to no avail. Henry Garnet reported to his Jesuit superiors in Rome that the hangman was most incompetent, the rope breaking twice under the strain of holding up Blessed Christopher's body before, on the third attempt, the whole ritual slaughter could properly begin.

BLESSED WILLIAM ANDLEBY

Born in Etton, near Beverley, Yorkshire circa 1552
Hanged, drawn and quartered at York on 4 July 1597
Beatified by Pope Pius XI on 15 December 1929

BORN AND BROUGHT up a Protestant, Blessed William graduated from St John's College, Cambridge, in 1572. Travelling to Flanders in order to support the Dutch Protestants in their fight against the Spaniards, he decided, out of curiosity, to visit Douai. There he met the college's founder, William Allen, who, over a number of meetings, convinced the future martyr of the truth of the Catholic Faith. Having become a Catholic, Blessed William entered the college being ordained a priest at Cateau-Cambrésis on 23 March 1577, St Ralph Sherwin being ordained at the same ceremony.

In early 1578 Blessed William set out for England, ministering principally in Yorkshire though he also reached Durham, Cambridgeshire and Lincolnshire. Along with another future martyr, Blessed Thomas Atkinson, Blessed William courageously but clandestinely found ways into Hull gaol where they ministered to prisoners there. Challoner wrote of him that 'Wonderful was the austerity of his life in frequent watchings, fastings, and continual prayer. He never spoke but where the honour of God and his neighbour's good required it ... even upon his journeys he was always in prayer, mental or vocal, with his soul so absorbed in God he often took no notice of those he met.' Perhaps this was how he came to be arrested? On 4 July Blessed William was martyred in York along with the *beati* Thomas Warcop, a layman who gave him refuge; Edward Fulthrop, a layman who was either reconciled to the Faith or converted by Blessed William; and Henry Abbot, who had been tricked by a Protestant minister into attempting to convert him.

1598

BLESSED PETER SNOW

Born in Cheshire or Ripon, date of birth unknown
Hanged, drawn and quartered at York on 15 June 1598
Beatified by Pope St John Paul II on 22 November 1987

RDAINED A PRIEST at Soissons in March or April 1591, Blessed Peter Snow left for the mission in England in mid-May of that year, heading to Yorkshire. Apart from one recorded sighting of him by a spy in 1593, Snow managed to allude the pursuivants for seven years until early May 1598 when he was arrested with his travelling companion, Blessed Ralph Grimston, on the road to York. The latter was charged with felony as he had 'lifted up his weapon' in an attempt to defend Father Snow, thus both Snow and Grimston were tried and condemned for treason.

Almost two hundred and fifty years later, in 1845, two human skulls were discovered under the stone floor of the chapel at Hazelwood Castle, near Tadcaster. At first these were thought to have been the relics of earlier English martyrs but in 1909, Dom Hildebrand Lane Fox, drawing on local traditions, concluded that these were the skulls of Blessed Peter Snow and Blessed Ralph Grimston. His conclusion was later corroborated by a forensic examination of the skulls in 1968 when it was shown that they were indeed of the time when the two martyrs were executed and showed markings that were consistent with the impaling of the heads on sharp objects.

From 1971 until 1996, Hazelwood Castle was owned by the Carmelite Order. In November 2006, the then Bishop of Leeds, Bishop Arthur Roche, enshrined the relics in the new High Altar of St Anne's Cathedral, Leeds. Before this, Bishop Roche allowed the two skulls to be examined by a forensic scientist in London who was able to reconstruct a facsimile image of how the martyrs probably appeared.

VENERABLE RICHARD HORNER

Born at Bolton-Bridge, Yorkshire, date of birth unknown
Hanged, drawn and quartered on 4 September 1598 at York
Declared Venerable by Pope Leo XIII in 1886

AVING STUDIED AT Douai College, the Venerable Richard Horner was ordained a priest in 1595, returning to England that year and ultimately being condemned for his priesthood.

1599

MATTHIAS HARRISON

Born in the Diocese of York, date of birth unknown
Hanged, drawn and quartered at York in 1599.

THE MOST ELUSIVE of Douai martyrs and sometimes confused with the Venerable James Harrison (d. 1602) all that is recorded of this martyr is
that he was ordained a priest in 1597, setting out for
England in the same year, and that he was martyred in
York in 1599.

1600

BLESSED CHRISTOPHER WHARTON

Born at Middleton, Yorkshire, in 1540
Hanged, drawn and quartered at York on 28 March
1600
Beatified by Pope St John Paul II on 22 November 1987

T SOME POINT after being made a Fellow of Trinity College, Oxford, Blessed Christopher became a Catholic, entering Douai College in Rheims at over forty years of age on 28 July 1583. He was ordained a priest by Cardinal Louis de Guise on 31 March 1584 but remained in Rheims for further study until 21 May 1586 when he set out for England, ministering in his native Yorkshire. Almost nothing is known of his ministry until his arrest at the house of Mrs Eleanor Hunt in the grounds of Sir William Ingleby's Ripley Castle. Both priest and his host were imprisoned in York Castle where one account records that during the weekly sermon given by a Protestant minister (on this occasion it was the Archbishop of York) to his captive Catholic congregation,

Blessed Christopher, along with another priest, rose to politely but clearly protest.

He was brought to trial at the Lenten Assizes of 1600 and professed that he was a priest but pointed out that the Statute of 1585 applied only to priests ordained after 1559, challenging the court to prove that he had been ordained after that date. This was to no avail as one of the judges knew the martyr from his time at Oxford and therefore was certain that he was not ordained by the crucial date. Sentence was passed and Blessed Christopher was martyred on Easter Friday 1600. Mrs Hunt, being spared execution for harbouring a priest, remained in prison until the end of her life.

BLESSED THOMAS SPROTT

Born in Skelsmergh, Westmorland, in 1571
Hanged, drawn and quartered in Lincoln on 1 July 1600
Beatified by Pope St John Paul II on 22 November 1987

RDAINED A PRIEST in the early months of 1596, Blessed Thomas set out for England in May of that year. He did not even get as far as England before being arrested as he was apprehended in the town of Brielle, one of three Dutch towns in English possession at that time. So it was as a prisoner that Blessed Thomas crossed the seas to England, being taken to the Bridewell prison in London.

Six months later he and nine other Catholic prisoners managed to escape, Blessed Thomas finding assistance from Fr Henry Garnett who then directed him out of London to a place of greater safety. Three years later it was his misfortune to have been staying with another priest, Blessed Thomas Hunt, at the Saracen's Head Inn in Lincoln when a mob invaded the premises searching for a notorious highwayman. All strangers were questioned and upon being searched they were found to be carrying rosary beads, holy oils and breviaries, thus they were arrested, strongly suspected of being Catholic priests.

At their trial the two men would not admit to being priests and, there being no conclusive proof that they were, the proceedings were in danger of stalling. The furious judge, Sir John Glanville, demanded that they confess but, with the priests refusing to do so, he instructed the jury to find them guilty in any case.

BLESSED EDWARD THWING

Born in Heworth, York, in 1565
Hanged, drawn and quartered at Lancaster on 26 July 1600.
Beatified by Pope St John Paul II on 22 November 1987

VEN AS A young man, Blessed Edward did not enjoy robust health, having to temporarily withdraw from the studies for priesthood that he had commenced in 1583 which he resumed in July 1585, proceeding to the English College, Rome, in November two years later. Poor health caused him to leave Rome in 1590, returning to Rheims and being ordained a priest at Laon on 20 December of the same year.

Because his health was so weak, it was thought best that Thwing should support the English mission by teaching Hebrew, Greek and rhetoric at the college in Rheims. This he did for seven years but in 1597 he was permitted to fulfil his desire of returning to his home country to support the Catholic mission in Lancashire.

In late March 1600 Blessed Edward was joined by Blessed Robert Nutter who had recently absconded from Wisbech Castle. The two were soon arrested and taken to Lancaster Castle. In prison, Blessed Edward wrote many letters to friends and family, including letters to the President of Douai College. In one he refers to himself as 'a prisoner for Christ', signing the letter 'from my prison paradise'; in another letter he declares that 'I shall if God make me worthy conclude an unhappy life with a most happy death.'

BLESSED ROBERT NUTTER

Born in Clitheroe, Lancashire, circa 1566
Hanged, drawn and quartered at Lancaster on 26 July 1600
Beatified by Pope St John Paul II on 22 November 1987

AVING ARRIVED AT Rheims with his elder brother, John, in August 1579, Blessed Robert was ordained a priest at Soissons on 22 December 1581, setting out for England less than two weeks later. For two years he secretly ministered over a large area of the south of England including Oxfordshire, Berkshire, Hampshire, Sussex and London. The government was well aware of him but could not catch him until February 1584 when he was arrested in Oxford and taken for torturing in the Tower. There, he was to join his brother, Blessed John Nutter, just a few days before his martyrdom.

Blessed Robert was to spend twelve months in the Tower before being suddenly released and banished from the realm. He made his way back to Rheims but this was only to start a highly dangerous operation of smuggling young men out of England so that they could enter the continental seminaries. By the end of the year he was heading once more towards England but his plans were thwarted when the vessel that he and three other priests were sailing in was intercepted by an English naval ship. All four priests were escorted, via Gravesend, to the Marshalsea. It is surprising that Blessed Robert was not executed at this time for breaking the order of banishment, but neither was he going to be a free man for by 1588 he had been transferred as a prisoner to Wisbech Castle in Cambridgeshire where he was to remain for the next twelve years, making his profession as a Dominican, having secretly corresponded with the Spanish Provincial, before other priests imprisoned with him at this time.

In March 1600 he and five other prisoners made their escape but after two months of ministry Nutter was caught, along with Blessed Thomas Thwing, in Lancashire, ultimately going to the gallows, according to one account, 'with as much cheerfulness and joy as if he had been going to a feast.'

BLESSED THOMAS PALASER

Born in Kirby Wiske, Yorkshire, circa 1570
Hanged, drawn and quartered at Durham on 8
September 1600
Beatified by Pope St John Paul II on 22 November
1987

OTH THE COLLEGES of Rheims and Valladolid can claim Blessed Thomas as their alumnus, the future martyr beginning his priestly studies at the former on 24 July 1592 before entering the latter on 3 January1593. He was ordained in 1596 returning later that year, as Fr Roland Connelly puts it, 'from a Spain hostile to Englishmen to an England hostile to Catholics.'

Caught almost immediately, his loyalty to the crown can be seen in his letter of 18 March 1587 to the Privy Council where he gave the government much military information about the intended Spanish invasion of England. Blessed Thomas, realizing that Topcliffe would certainly interrogate and torture him, miraculously managed to make his escape and, making his way to the north of England, ministered around Durham and North Yorkshire for three years until 24 June 1600 when in the house of Blessed John Norton and his wife at Ravensworth, Co Durham, he was once again arrested, items for the celebration of Mass and Catholic books being discovered at the house. As well as Blessed John Norton, Blessed John Talbot who had been present in the Norton's house at the time of the raid, was also martyred with their priest on the feast day of the Nativity of the Blessed Virgin Mary 1600. Blessed John's wife, Margaret, being with child at the time, was reprieved.

1601

BLESSED JOHN PIBUSH

Born at Thirsk, Yorkshire, date of birth unknown.
Hanged, drawn and quartered at St Thomas's
Waterings, Camberwell, 18 February 1601
Beatified by Pope Pius XI on 15 December 1929

BLESSED JOHN PIBUSH entered the English College at Rheims on 4 August 1580 and was ordained a priest on 14 March 1587, departing for England in January of the following year. Nothing is known of his ministry until his arrest at the Hart Inn at Moreton-in-Marsh, Gloucestershire, in 1593, whereupon he was sent to London to be incarcerated at the Gatehouse at Westminster. After a year Pibush was tried at the Gloucester Assizes for being a priest, yet he was not sentenced but taken to Gloucester gaol from where he escaped on 19 February 1594.

He was not free for much more than a day when he was recaptured at Matson and returned to Gloucester gaol from where he was transported to Marshalsea, London, and again tried at Westminster on 1 July 1595 and sen-

tenced to death. Blessed John was held at first at Marshalsea before being taken to the King's Bench prison where
he was imprisoned for five years, contracting tuberculosis
during this time. From prison he was able to send out a
letter, the original and an English translation by Henry
Garnet SJ, which includes these lines, were sent to the
Jesuit General in Rome:

> Those who purpose to come to this country and to
> work profitably therein must bring along with them
> vigorous souls and mortified bodies. They must
> forgo all pleasure and renounce every game but that
> of football, which is made up of pushes and kicks
> and requires constant effort unless one would be
> trampled under foot; and in this game they have to
> risk their lives in order to save souls. On my return
> to England I found that it was one huge prison for
> all who, like us, profess the true faith.

And, of his condition as he wrote, he related, clothed in
'filth, lice and fleas',

> Sir, sickness hath made me so absolutely a conquest
> of my bodily health that friends and acquaintances
> coming to the place where I live, and sitting in my
> company, have asked, who is he? I have lived reft of
> holy rites, singled from the society of men, seques-
> tered from my friends, debarred of student's com-
> forts, punished with my company as S. Chrysostom
> with the soldiers that carried him into exile. Yet eight
> year's imprisonment and 43 years our common
> calamity I hope shall not discourage us. For my own
> part I account mine as but yesterday begun ...

The death sentence being ultimately carried out with just
one day's notice at St Thomas's Waterings, the St Thomas
of the name being the martyred Archbishop of Canterbury.

BLESSED MARK BARKWORTH

Born in Searby, Lincolnshire, in 1570
Hanged, drawn and quartered at Tyburn, London
on 27 February 1601
Beatified by Pope Pius XI on 15 December 1929

TANDING BESIDE THE gallows as St Anne Line's lifeless body hung, Blessed Mark, the first English Benedictine martyr of the Reformation, approached and kissed the hem of her dress and her hand too, saying 'Thou has got the start of us, sister, but we will follow thee as quickly as we may', after which he and a Jesuit priest, Blessed Roger Filcock, were hanged, drawn and quartered. So ended Blessed Mark's earthly life in a manner that had been foretold in his childhood by a seer, a prophecy that so alarmed his parents that they dispatched their son to Oxford University in the hope that a good education would protect him from such a fate.

While there is no record of him at Oxford, his matriculation at Douai on 5 October 1594 is certain, Blessed Mark having become a Catholic during travels on the continent and visiting the English College and deciding to stay. From Douai he was sent to Valladolid in 1596 where he was ordained a priest three years later, then returning to the mission in England but not before having given thought to becoming a Benedictine. He was advised to first try his vocation as a secular priest but, having stopped at the monastery of Irache in Navarre, he was given permission to profess himself as a member of the Benedictines should he find himself in danger of death.

Very soon after arriving in England, Blessed Mark was arrested, despite trying to hide himself under the alias of

Lambert. After incarceration in the Bridewell prison, trial and sentencing, the day of execution may have been decided in order to make the deaths of the Catholics a distraction from the execution of the Earl of Essex, the queen's favourite, ten days later, a Catholic martyrdom not having been carried out at Tyburn since the death of St Robert Southwell in 1595. On his way to Tyburn, Blessed Mark sang out the Easter anthem, *Hæc dies, quam fecit Dominus, exultemus et lætemur in ea* ('This is the day, the Lord has made, let us rejoice and be glad in it.'), and, dressed as a monk, his head shaven with a tonsure as a monk, he used his speech to remind the onlookers that it had been his order that Pope Gregory the Great had sent to England to proclaim the Gospel. The hangman was particularly brutal with Blessed Mark, cutting the rope from which his body swung almost immediately after the cart on which the martyr stood had been drawn away. Blessed Mark came to his feet and attempted to grapple with the knife wielding executioner until, succumbing, he cried out 'O Lord, O Lord, O Lord!' while Blessed Roger Filcock encouraged him in his agony. When the bloody rites had been accomplished the quartered bodies of neither the priests were sent to the city gates or London bridge but were buried beside the scaffold, although at least some parts were retrieved by night.

BLESSED ROGER FILCOCK

Born in Sandwich, Kent, circa 1570
Hanged, drawn and quartered at Tyburn, London
on 27 February 1601
Beatified by Pope St John Paul II on 22 November 1987

AVING ARRIVED AT the English College in Rheims on 15 June 1588, Blessed Roger was to be part of the first cohort of students to study at the newly founded college in Valladolid, entering the college on 20 February 1591 and being ordained a priest there six years later. Although he wanted to become a Jesuit, his superior, Fr Henry Garnet thought it prudent that he experienced some years on the English mission first. In December 1597 he set sail for England from Bilbao to Calais and then on to the Kent coast. The journey was made more difficult when the ship to Calais was pursued by Dutch vessels, some on board the French boat jumping ship to escape, but Blessed Roger was arrested, somehow managing to escape.

For the next two years he ministered around London, being admitted to the Society of Jesus in around 1600. He was about to travel to Flanders for his novitiate at the time of his arrest in a house of the widow St Anne Line, the priest having been betrayed by a former student from Valladolid. At Blessed Roger's trial, the mere suspicion of his being a priest was enough for the death sentence to be pronounced by the recorder, the martyr having refused a jury trial as he did not want the twelve innocent men to be guilty of his blood. It was Blessed Mark Barkworth who wrote of Blessed Roger as 'always one of my chiefest and dearest friends, as well as formerly when he was at liberty as now in prison. A man exceedingly humble and of

extraordinary patience, piety and charity.' Watching
Barkworth die, Filcock cried out, 'I desire to be dissolved
and to be with Christ!' Fr Garnet considered that Blessed
Roger had been 'twice martyred' for having to watch the
horrendous death of his friend before his own.

BLESSED THURSTON HUNT

Born at Carlton Hall, Rothwell, Yorkshire, in 1555
Hanged, drawn and quartered at Lancaster on 3
April 1601
Beatified by Pope St John Paul II on 22 November 1987

RDAINED A PRIEST on 20 April 1585, less than
two years after arriving in Rheims, Blessed
Thurston returned to England. He successfully
evaded detection through fifteen years of ministry in
Lancashire, Yorkshire and Cheshire. He would have been
able to work for longer had he not led a group in a failed
attempt to rescue another priest, Blessed Robert Middleton, during his transfer from Preston to Lancaster Castle,
Blessed Thurston firing a gun in self-defence, swords and
rocks being used by others. As if this was not alarming
enough for the authorities, letters found on Blessed
Thurston, including an open letter to the queen warning
her of an alleged Puritan plot to depose her, caused the
two priests to be taken to London for further questioning.
From his cell in the Gatehouse, Blessed Thurston wrote
another declaration that the queen's life was in danger and
hoping that the government would show both him and
Blessed Robert clemency for having alerted them to a plot.
The response was simply to return the two to Preston for
trial and execution.

Blessed Robert Middleton

Born at York in 1570
Hanged, drawn and quartered at Lancaster on 3
April 1601
Beatified by Pope St John Paul II on 22 November 1987

STUDENT OF BOTH Douai (1594–97) and the
English College, Rome (1597–98), Blessed Robert
had been reconciled to the Catholic Church three
years after the death of his aunt, St Margaret Clitherow in
1586. Ordained a priest on 4 January 1598 he left Rome
on 20 April of the same year. In England his mission field
was the north of England, working firstly in Yorkshire
before his arrest in Ripon at Christmastide 1599 and his
subsequent escape from prison in York, and then in
Lancashire where, on 30 September 1600, he was caught
again, this time near Preston. After imprisonment and
examination in Preston he was transferred to Lancaster,
and it was on the way to Lancaster that Blessed Thurston
Hunt and his band attempted to free him.

Transferred to London, Blessed Robert made his profession as a Jesuit whilst held in the Gatehouse prison, Fr
Henry Garnett accepting him into the Society. Returned
to Lancaster, the two priests died having absolved each
other and both dressed in their cassocks.

1602

VENERABLE JAMES HARRISON

Born in the Diocese of Lichfield, date of birth unknown.
Hanged, drawn and quartered at York, 22 March 1602

THE FIRST RECORD of the Venerable James Harrison is of his studies and subsequent ordination in Rheims in 1583, leaving for England the following year. The extent of his labours in his home country are known only to God for the next extant information about him is that he was arrested at the house of one Anthony Battie who, for the crime of giving the priest shelter, was also hanged, drawn and quartered with Harrison. Challoner notes that Harrison's head was somehow procured and venerated by the Franciscans at Douai.

VENERABLE THOMAS TICHBORNE

Born Hartley, Hampshire, in 1567.
Hanged, drawn and quartered at Tyburn, London,
20 April 1602

RDAINED A PRIEST in Rome on Ascension Day 1592 (17 May), having previously studied at Rheims, Thomas Tichborne returned to England in 1594 and worked in the mission until he was captured in 1601. Whilst being transferred between prisons a courageous young Catholic, the Venerable Thomas Hackshot overpowered Tichborne's guard, allowing him to escape. But Hackshot was himself arrested, imprisoned, tortured and finally executed along with the Venerable Nicholas Tichborne, a relative of Thomas, who had also conspired to set Thomas free.

Thomas Tichborne's dearly bought freedom did not last long as he was spotted in the street by an apostate priest who, recognising him, shouted 'A priest! A priest! Stop the priest!', thus causing the martyr to be arrested, tried and condemned to death, suffering alongside Blessed Robert Watkinson and Blessed Francis Page SJ.

Blessed Robert Watkinson

Born at Hemingborough, Yorkshire, in 1579
Hanged, drawn and quartered at Tyburn, London,
20 April 1602
Beatified by Pope Pius XI on 15 December 1929

REPARED FOR PRIESTHOOD at both Rome and Douai, Watkinson was ordained at Arras on the Feast of the Annunciation 1602, returning to England at the beginning of April. He was in noticeably poor health at this time and, while walking through the streets of London, saw a poor man to whom he gave some coins, the man saying to him, "Jesus bless you, sir, you seem to be sick and troubled with many infirmities; but be of good cheer, for within these four days you shall be cured of all." These extraordinary words were proved true for the very next day Watkinson was arrested, through the treachery of an apostate student of Douai, and, on the following Tuesday, executed at Tyburn along with Blessed Francis Page and the Venerable Thomas Tichborne.

Blessed Francis Page

Born in Antwerp, born circa 1575
Hanged, drawn and quartered at Tyburn, London
on 20 April 1602
Beatified by Pope Pius XI on 15 December 1929

T WAS HIS love for a young lady that drew Blessed Francis Page towards becoming a Catholic, the lady in question insisting that her suitor had to be Catholic to win her hand. Unfortunately for her, the more that Page discovered about the Catholic Church the more he felt that God was calling him to the priesthood.

Francis Page was born in Antwerp of affluent English parents. He returned to England to study law and it was the daughter of a Catholic lawyer who attracted his attentions. Seeking instruction in the Faith, Page turned to the Jesuit, Fr John Gerard. He became devoted to him and, when Gerard was arrested and imprisoned in the Tower of London, Page stood outside the prison almost daily, gaining the attention of the authorities and then finding himself briefly under arrest. Page had become convinced of his calling and travelled to Douai College to train to be a priest.

Francis Page was ordained at Arras in April 1600 and soon returned to England, at least once avoiding capture by a hair's breadth as he was about to say Mass in the house of St Anne Line on the Feast of Candlemas, 1601. Becoming aware of the fast-approaching danger, Page removed his vestments and sat in the congregation as though he too was awaiting the arrival of a priest. For this and for her many mercies to priests, St Anne was hanged just three weeks later.

Just over a year later Page was captured thanks to the greed of a lady who was happy to receive the rewards given to those who betrayed priests. Having been recognised, Page tried to take refuge in an inn, but the innkeeper held him captive until the authorities arrived. After being condemned to death, Page was permitted to join a Jesuit in an adjoining cell and took vows as a Jesuit himself, which he proudly proclaimed to the crowds who witnessed his death.

1603

BLESSED WILLIAM RICHARDSON

Born in Wales circa 1572
Hanged, drawn and quartered at Tyburn, London
on 17 February 1603
Beatified by Pope Pius XI on 15 December 1929

THE FINAL CATHOLIC martyr of the reign of Queen Elizabeth I arrived in Rheims in July 1592 and was quickly sent on to the English College in Valladolid, arriving there on 23 December of the same year. He also studied in Seville, returning to England as a priest in 1600, using the alias of Henderson.

Nothing is known of his ministry until his betrayal and arrest at Clement's Inn, one of the Inns of Court in London, on 12 February 1603. After one week in Newgate, Blessed Willliam was tried before the lord chief justice, Sir John Popham, and martyred the very next morning, by various accounts he went cheerfully to his death. Just over one month later, the queen was dead.

1604

BLESSED JOHN SUGAR

Born at Wombourne, near Wolverhampton, Staffordshire in 1558
Hanged, drawn and quartered at Warwick on 16 July 1604
Beatified by Pope St John Paul II on 22 November 1987

LTHOUGH A MEMBER of St Mary's Hall of Oriel College, Oxford, Blessed John Sugar left the university without a degree, becoming Vicar of Cannock in Staffordshire. Exactly when he became a Catholic is unknown but it is recorded that he entered the English College at Douai on 25 June 1599, being ordained a priest on 21 April 1601 and setting out for England on 4 October of the same year. According to Bishop Challoner, who relied on 'an old manuscript now lost', Blessed John ministered in the Midlands and 'travelled afoot very much' throughout Warwickshire, Staffordshire and Worcestershire.

Blessed John was apprehended at Rowington in Warwickshire on 8 July 1603 along with Blessed Robert Grissold, a layman who was assisting him. Blessed John managed to briefly outwit the pursuivants but he was tracked down on the open road, both men being incarcerated in Warwick. Although found guilty of being a priest, sentence was delayed while the new king, James I, was petitioned for a Royal Pardon, it being thought that he was most reluctant to persecute Catholics. During the following twelve months strenuous attempts were made to persuade Blessed John to renounce the Faith. On 13 July 1604, no pardon having been received, he was sentenced to death. On the morning of his execution, according to Bishop Challoner's manuscript, he comforted the faithful who visited him saying, 'Be ye all merry, for we have not occasion of sorrow but of joy; for although I shall have a sharp dinner, yet I trust in Jesus Christ I shall have a most sweet supper.'

1606

BLESSED EDWARD OLDCORNE

Born in York in 1561
Hanged, drawn and quartered at Redhill, Worcester,
on 7 April 1606.
Beatified by Pope Pius XI on 15 December 1929.

NE OF THE most celebrated relics of the Douai martyrs is from the body of Blessed Edward Oldcorne and is in the keeping of Stonyhurst College: it is one his eyes. He first saw the light of day in York 1561, born the son of a bricklayer, John Oldcorne, and his wife Elizabeth. Having studied medicine as a young man he decided to offer himself for the priesthood, first entering the college at Rheims on 12 August 1581 and then being sent on to Rome the following February, being ordained a priest in the Lateran on 23 August 1587. On the feast of the Assumption, 1588, he and John Gerard entered the Society of Jesus, being immediately sent to England, sailing across the English Chanel in late October or early November and landing in East Anglia, Oldcorne then heading for London.

From London Blessed Edward, using the alias of Hall, embarked on a missionary tour of the midlands accompanied by the Jesuit superior in England, Henry Garnet. Basing himself at Hindlip House near Worcester, the home of the Catholic Habington family, he ministered throughout the surrounding area becoming known for his engaging preaching. Fr John Gerard was to remark that Hindlip became like 'one of our houses in some foreign country—so many Catholics flocked there to receive the sacraments, or to hear him preach or to get his advice.' Fr Garnet adds, 'It was his work to bring many to the faith in this and neighbouring counties, to support the wavering and lift up the fallen, and to station priests in many places.'

In 1601 Blessed Edward made a pilgrimage to St Winifride's Well in North Wales seeking a cure for cancer of his throat. His prayers were granted and in September 1605 he audaciously yet secretly returned with a group of pilgrims to give thanks for his healing. Unfortunately, the group included at least one man who was involved in the Gunpowder Plot and later this trip was used as evidence to implicate innocent participants.

For seventeen years Blessed Edward cared for the Catholics of his area, not without occasional narrow escapes from pursuivants, but he was to embroiled in the reaction to the Gunpowder Plot of 1605 thanks to the betrayal of Humphrey Littleton, a man imprisoned on a charge of harbouring some of the conspirators as they fled the reach of justice. Littleton hoped to save himself by informing the Privy Council of Blessed Edward's presence at Hindlip and suggesting that Henry Garnet might also be found there too. On 20 January 1606, with the property surrounded by a hundred men, a systematic and forensic search of the house began, a search that followed careful instructions from London. Blessed Edward and Fr Garnet were hiding in a small priest hole hidden by the chimney. They had a small store of food and, through an ingeniously concealed reed in the masonry, they could receive warm broths from the mistress of the house's room. There was even a small outlet through which they could urinate. It was cramped, though, Garnet later recalling that both men suffered from swollen legs yet they 'were merry and content within' and heard each other's general confessions.

Three days later St Nicholas Owen, who had built a number of hiding places for priests at Hindlip and other houses, and Blessed Ralph Ashley emerged starving from their hiding places—they only had had a single apple between them—and were caught. The search of the house was redoubled: floorboards were ripped up, wainscoting torn down and lines of holes drilled in the floors, 'books, massing stuff and popish trumpery' being found. On 27 January Henry Garnet and Blessed Edward were also discovered, the lack of a close stool finally forcing them out of their hiding place.

Blessed Edward was taken to London and first imprisoned in the Gatehouse and then in the Tower where he was tortured, being racked for five hours a day over five consecutive days. Garnet was taken to the Tower too and housed in a cell next to Blessed Edward, even being shown 'a cranny in the top of the door' through which the two of them could converse: all a ploy by the authorities who had hidden eavesdroppers within earshot, noting everything down. Blessed Edward steadfastly denied all knowledge of the plot and was sent back to Worcester for trial at the Lenten assizes where he was found guilty of inviting Garnet, who was considered a traitor, to seek refuge in the house; that he had helped hide two conspirators associated with the Gunpowder Plot; and that he had thought the Plot a good endeavour. On the scaffold he prayed for the

king and royal family, forgave the judge and jury who
found him guilty and Humphrey Littleton, who was
executed with him and publicly confessed that he had
wrongfully accused Blessed Edward of association with
the conspiracy. Blessed Ralph Ashley was also martyred
on the same day at Red Hill. The blow with which the
executioner beheaded Blessed Edward's body was so great
that one of his eyes flew out, being retrieved by a Catholic
sympathiser standing nearby.

1607

BLESSED ROBERT DRURY

Born in Buckinghamshire in 1568
Hanged, drawn and quartered at Tyburn, London,
on 26 February 1607
Beatified by Pope St John Paul II on 22 November 1987

N 1 APRIL 1588 Blessed Robert, born of a gentry family in Buckinghamshire, arrived for two years of study at Rheims after which he was sent on to the newly founded English College at Valladolid, being ordained a priest there by the Bishop of León in 1595. Returning to England in the autumn of the same year, Blessed Robert was assisted by the Jesuit priest, John Gerard, and given lodgings in London in the house of the future martyr, St Anne Line. In his biography, John Gerard recalls that Blessed Robert 'was well born and well educated ... and he could move about in the best society without suspicion. I gave him an introduction to my friends among the gentry and he was a great assistance to them'.

Blessed Robert was among those who appealed against the controversial appointment of George Blackwell as

Archpriest in England, earning for himself a temporary
suspension from ministry for his troubles, and he was
among the priests who in January 1603 protested their
allegiance to the queen in the forlorn hope that this would
be enough to appease the authorities and quench the
persecution of Catholics. After some years more of hidden
ministry, Blessed Robert was arrested on 10 February 1607
along with another priest, William Davies, and some laity
in the London house of the Catholic Stansby family. Only
the two priests were taken to Newgate prison, tried and
condemned. Both could have saved their lives if they took
the oath of allegiance, but as this denied the temporal power
of the pope, neither could take the oath. Davies, perhaps
due to advanced age, was ultimately spared and banished
from the realm—Blessed Robert was dragged to his death
at Tyburn alongside thirty-two thieves and murderers.

1608

BLESSED MATTHEW FLATHERS

Born in Weston, Yorkshire, in 1560
Hanged, drawn and quartered at York on 21 March
1608
Beatified by Pope St John Paul II on 22 November 1987

A GRADUATE OF UNIVERSITY COLLEGE, Oxford, Blessed Matthew was about forty years old when he entered the English College at Douai on 18 August 1604, being confirmed there on 22 March of the following year. The very next year he was ordained a priest at Arras on the Feast of the Annunciation, setting out for England on 30 June. This was 1606 and the Gunpowder Plot of the previous year had fired up the state in its zeal to hunt priests, a proclamation banishing them from the realm having just been promulgated when Blessed Matthew arrived in England. He was caught almost immediately, tried and condemned but, through an act of clemency, he was exiled for the rest of his life.

Having reached Douai, the future martyr began his homeward journey almost immediately but was arrested again almost as soon in August 1607 at Upsall Castle in Yorkshire. Blessed Matthew was one of three priests present at the castle at the time that the priest hunter Sir Stephen Procter forced his way in. One priest escaped, but the other, Father William Mush, was taken along with Lady Constable, the woman who had taken them in, and Blessed Matthew to York where they were brought to trial at the Lenten Assizes and condemned to death. Ultimately only Blessed Matthew was martyred, Fr Mush managing to escape and Lady Constable being reprieved but left in prison indefinitely.

BLESSED GEORGE GERVASE

Born in Bosham, Sussex, in 1569
Hanged, drawn and quartered at Tyburn, London,
on 11 April 1608
Beatified by Pope Pius XI on 15 December 1929

RELATED THROUGH HIS mother to the martyr Blessed Edward Shelley, it is probable that Blessed George was brought up as a Catholic. It seems that he was orphaned at a young age and may have served with Sir Francis Drake as part of his 1595 failed mission to the West Indies. Adventure attracted him and, on his return, Blessed George went to Flanders, serving in the Spanish army after which he made his way to Douai to study for the priesthood, being ordained at Cambrai in 1603.

In 1604 Blessed George returned to England, ministering in different areas of the country until his arrest in 1606. A spell in prison ensued, followed by banishment. Returning to Douai he decided to go on pilgrimage to Rome. On his return he became a novice at the newly founded

Benedictine house, St Gregory's in Douai. He was back in England in 1607, ministering in London where he was arrested just two months after his return. Blessed George was condemned to death for refusing to take the oath of allegiance, though professing loyalty to the king, and for being a priest. It is almost certain that he made his final vows as a Benedictine before his martyrdom and is regarded as the proto-martyr of St Gregory's, Douai, though Douai College itself was also keen to claim the martyr as a member of the secular clergy.

BLESSED ROGER CADWALLADOR

Born in Stretton, Herefordshire, in 1566
Hanged, drawn and quartered in Leominster,
Herefordshire, on 27 August 1610
Beatified by Pope St John Paul II on 22 November 1987

LESSED ROGER WAS the eldest son and heir to a Catholic family 'of substance'. He arrived at the English College, Rheims, on 26 March 1590 being ordained a deacon there before continuing his formation in Valladolid from January 1593. He was swiftly ordained a priest by the Bishop of Zamora in the same year and returned to England, ministering in Herefordshire for the next sixteen years.

Not long before the death of Queen Elizabeth I, Blessed Roger was one of thirteen signatories to a declaration known as the Protestation of Allegiance of 30 January 1603. Acknowledging the queen as the legitimate sovereign, those who signed this declaration promised her obedience in temporal matters as far as the law of God permitted, to defend England against invasions and to reject conspiracies against her, all of this while also declaring their allegiance to the Bishop of Rome. It was a brave stance but was rejected, those who physically presented it being imprisoned.

Blessed Roger was arrested near Hereford on 8 April 1610 and examined by the Bishop of Hereford. After refusing to take the Oath of Allegiance he was clapped in unusually heavy irons and cast into Hereford gaol. Shackled, he was transferred on foot to Leominster gaol where one visitor found him still in chains: shaking them, he compared them to the sound of the little bells on the biblical High Priest's robes.

On the day of his martyrdom Blessed Roger put on new clothes that a friend had sent to him and he sent some money to the porter of the gaol, keeping a little aside to give to the man who led the horse that was to drag his hurdle. As with other martyrs, he was offered his life if he would take the Oath of Allegiance: refusing, he was left to the ineptitude of an unskilled executioner.

BLESSED GEORGE NAPPER

Born in Oxford in 1550
Hanged, drawn and quartered in Oxford on 9 November 1610
Beatified by Pope Pius XI on 15 December 1929

RELATED, THROUGH HIS mother, to Cardinal William Peto, Blessed George Napper (or Napier) was educated at Corpus Christi College, Oxford, until he was expelled in 1568 due to his staunch Catholicism. It is not until 1580 that more is known about him, due to his being imprisoned for rejecting the royal supremacy, a stance that he recanted nine years later, thus earning his release. But he returned to his former beliefs and, in 1596, entered Douai, being ordained a priest and, in 1603, setting out for England, working for seven years in Oxfordshire.

Early in the morning of 19 July 1610 Blessed George was arrested in the fields of Kirtlington, a small village near Oxford. When searched, he was found to be carrying his breviary and Holy Oils, though the officers failed to find the pyx that he was also carrying, containing two consecrated hosts, and a small reliquary. Friends sought his release but, whilst in prison, the priest reconciled a condemned man to the Faith, thus sealing his own fate. A fellow prisoner held with Blessed George wrote of him, 'His charity was great, for if any poor prisoner wanted either meat to fill him or clothes to cover him he would rather be cold himself than they should.' adding that the martyr was 'remarkably laborious in gaining souls for God.'

BLESSED THOMAS SOMERS

Born in Westmoreland, date of birth unknown
Hanged, drawn and quartered at Tyburn, London,
10 December 1610
Beatified by Pope Pius XI on 15 December 1929

EW, IF ANY, of the English martyrs can have spent the night before their deaths in a manner like Blessed Thomas Somers enjoyed. We may know little about his life beyond his nickname as the 'parish priest of London' and his ministry to plague victims, but about his trial and death, thanks to the ministrations of a Spanish noblewoman, we know some surprising details.

Having spent some years as a school master, Blessed Thomas entered Douai, returning to England as a priest in 1606. Challoner held that, after some time of ministry, working under the alias of Wilson, Blessed Thomas was arrested and banished from the realm but soon returned and was rearrested, tried and sentenced to death, being tried and executed with St John Roberts, a Benedictine monk who gave a fiery defence of himself and his companion, rebuking the Bishop of London for sitting with civil judges at their trial. As the death sentence was pronounced, Luisa de Carvajal, a Spanish noblewoman known to Roberts, records that she 'prostrated herself before their lucky feet and kissed them, telling them how I was brimming with jealousy for their happy fate.' Her next act was to send the priests some pear tartlets, a small act of kindness considering what happened next.

On the night before St John and Blessed Thomas were to be martyred, Luisa paid the jailor of Newgate a large bribe so that her and two companions could give the priests, with at least twenty other imprisoned Catholics, a last supper. With Luisa sitting at the head of the table, St John and Blessed Thomas either side of her, the assembly feasted. Unsurprisingly, when King James came to hear of these goings on some months later, he was incandescent with rage, summoning the jailor to examination by the Star Chamber.

On the day of their martyrdom, the priests died with sixteen criminals, being allowed to die by hanging before being butchered. Their heads were taken to London Bridge to be displayed, their bodies were buried at Tyburn but Catholic sympathisers recovered the quartered bodies and Luisa arranged for a carriage to bring the remains to her house in the Barbican. The carriage was stopped and inspected by the night guard, who beat a hasty retreat when confronted by the terrifying spectacle of one of St

John Robert's legs falling out of the vehicle. Half of Blessed Thomas's chest also seems to have been lost at this point. What remained was delivered safely to Luisa who later wrote to the Marquess of Caracena,

> I considered myself fortunate to have these guests, and to be able to serve them in such great need, being unable to find a nook or cranny that was halfway safe to put them in. In order to prepare them, one arm with half a chest and its back was placed on the floor, and the other with the other half. It was an extraordinary sight and cause for much prayer to see these so frail weapons that had fought without frailty but with conviction. They flew up to heaven, where they increased the number of intercessions, making my house happy with such remains.

Bit by bit, but carefully and reverently, Luisa's 'guests' left her home to find their way to reliquaries across the continent.

1612

BLESSED RICHARD NEWPORT
(ALSO KNOWN AS RICHARD SMITH)

Born in Harringworth, Northamptonshire, in 1572
Hanged, drawn and quartered at Tyburn, London,
on 30 May 1612
Beatified by Pope Pius XI on 15 December 1929

IN ORDER TO protect his family, and himself, Richard Newport was known as Richard Smith during his preparation for the priesthood. After initial studies at Douai College, Newport was sent to the English College, Rome, being ordained a priest in 1599. His was going to be an itinerant ministry as, in the course of his twelve to thirteen years of priesthood he was captured and arrested twice, being banished to the continent on both occasions, before his final trial. On the first expulsion from England, Blessed Richard took the opportunity to make a pilgrimage to Rome, praying for his beloved and beleaguered country at the tombs of the Apostles.

On being arrested and imprisoned for the third time, Blessed Richard found himself incarcerated with the Benedictine priest, Blessed William Scott. Both were brought before the Lord Mayor of London, the Bishop of London and various magistrates where Blessed Richard defended himself against the charge of treason and not complying with his banishment by reminding the judge that Christ had instructed his Apostles to 'Go, and teach all nations.': this was why he had no alternative but to return to England. Giving his final blessing to the onlooking crowd, he prepared to die along with Blessed William Scott.

Present at the execution was the French manservant of Luisa de Carvajal (see entry on Blessed Thomas Somers), Lemeteliel, whose task was to observe where the bodies of the martyrs were buried. He noted that they were buried in a wide ditch as deep as a man near the gallows. Being summer, the nights were short so Luisa knew that in order to retrieve the remains under the cover of darkness, many hands were needed. It was not difficult for her to drum up support from friends at the Spanish embassy as Blessed Thomas had acted as confessor there. It was also not difficult to identify the quartered bodies as they had been buried beneath sixteen or more corpses of criminals who had been hanged, but not quartered, after the martyrs' deaths, the felons' executions following the 'traitors' precisely so that the whole bodies could be used to cover the quartered ones. It must have been grisly work, but the martyrs' bodies were exhumed and then fitted into pouches made up of Luisa's old bedsheets and, at great danger to all involved, were transported to the Spanish noble woman's house in Spitalfields. At the house the relics were carried to Luisa's chapel, the passages and stairs strewn with flowers, and placed 'on a carpet in front of the altar and covered with large piece of red material that was new, with lots of sweet-smelling flowers on top. On bended knee,' recorded Luisa, 'we offered up prayer.'

The next day Luisa wiped clean the relics and coated them in strong smelling spices before depositing them in leaden boxes, two of which were taken to the Spanish ambassador's home at Gondomar in Galicia.

SAINT JOHN ALMOND

Born in Allerton, Lancashire, in 1567
Hanged, drawn and quartered at Tyburn, London,
on 5 December 1612
Beatified by Pope Pius XI on 15 December 1929
Canonized by Pope St Paul VI on 25 October 1970

PARTICULARLY GIFTED THEOLOGIAN and orator, St John was ordained in Rome in 1601 and crowned his studies in Rome with a brilliant disputation that was praised by the great ecclesiastical historian, Cardinal Baronius, who presided over the academic feat. From Rome St John journeyed to Douai where he stayed for a month until setting out for England in November 1602. Back in England St John was able to work until his arrest in March 1612 when he was brought to the Bishop of London for examination. He refused to sign the Oath of Allegiance but declared that he was happy to swear 'so much allegiance to King James (whom I pray God to bless now and evermore) as he, or any Christian king, could expect by the law of nature, the law of God, or the positive law of the true Church, be it which it will, ours or yours.'

After nine months imprisonment in Newgate he was brought to trial as a seminary priest and sentenced to death, but not before taunting the Anglican bishops present at his trial to go back to their wives and children. At Tyburn he was permitted to address the crowd and he answered objections that were put to him. He then emptied his pockets of such silver coins as he had and threw them into the crowd, addressing them finally with these words:

> One hour overtaketh another, and though never so long, at last cometh death. And yet not death; for death is the gate of life unto us whereby we enter into everlasting blessedness. And life is death to those who do not provide for death, for they are ever tossed and troubled with vexations, miseries and wickedness. To use this life well is the pathway through death to everlasting life.

Having asked for a handkerchief to cover his face, the martyr died with the name of Jesus on his lips and in his heart.

Meanwhile, underneath the scaffold, a French manservant had been sent by Luisa de Carvajal (see entry on Blessed Thomas Somers) to catch on brilliant-white cloths any drops of the martyr's blood that might fall between the rough boards of the staging, and to observe where St John's body was buried. On the night after the execution Luisa organized a group of men to exhume the body, the only difficulty that they ran into was another group of relic hunters who had the same aim. Luisa prevailed and had St John's body brought to her house to be preserved, prepared as relics and revered.

1616

BLESSED THOMAS ATKINSON

Born in the East Riding of Yorkshire, circa 1546
Hanged, drawn and quartered at York on 11 March
1616
Beatified by Pope St John Paul II on 22 November 1987

LESSED THOMAS ATKINSON must have been about forty years of age by the time that he arrived at the English College in Rheims, being ordained a priest at Laon on 11 June 1588 and setting out to England the following November.

He returned to his home county, working with Blessed William Andleby until the latter's arrest in 1597. More is known about Blessed Thomas's ministry than that of many of the Douai martyrs thanks to the memoirs of Lady Grace Babthorpe of Osgody in Howdenshire, written in 1620. In them she recalls the priest:

> For several years, he travelled on foot, enduring all weathers, and many times when he had a weary and wet day, the houses to which he went could not receive him, but that he must stay in some out-

house or corner, he being both wet and cold, and in
time of frost and snow, to such time as the owners
of the houses could for their safety receive him in.

At some point in his sixties Blessed Thomas broke his leg,
it being then badly set by an incompetent doctor. After
this he was constrained to use a horse to get around until
his arrest when visiting a Catholic family at Willitoft, near
Howden. He was tied to a horse and transported to prison
in York where he steadfastly refused to admit that he was
a priest lest the family in whose home he had been arrested
should incur the weight of the law. At his trial the only
incriminating evidence that could be produced was his
rosary beads and grains of incense that he was discovered
to have been carrying when he was searched: this was
enough for him to be found guilty of being a priest.

BLESSED JOHN THULES

Born at Whalley, Lancashire, in December 1568
Hanged, drawn and quartered at Lancaster on 18
March 1616
Beatified by Pope St John Paul II on 22 November 1987

RRIVING AT RHEIMS on 28 May 1583, Blessed
John Thules was only fifteen years old. Seven
years later he was sent to the English College,
Rome, and was ordained a priest at the Lateran Basilica
on 28 March 1592 having received a canonical dispensation due to being ten months underage. In April of the
same year he returned to England and was already captured in Northumberland in July but he managed to
escape. Reports of his presence in Essex and Lancashire
exist for 1605 and 1610 respectively but it was to be five

more years before he was finally arrested on 29 September 1615, being imprisoned in Lancaster gaol with a Catholic weaver named Roger Wrenno, in whose Chorley house the priest had been staying. Not long before their trial at the Lenten Assizes of 1616 the two managed to escape during a mass breakout at the gaol but, losing their sense of direction, they thought that had managed to walk a long distance from Lancaster but had, in fact, managed to walk a circular route that brought them perilously near where they had started from, thus they were rearrested, tried, condemned, martyred and beatified together in 1987.

BLESSED THOMAS MAXFIELD

Born at Maer Hall, Enville, in Staffordshire, in 1585
Hanged, drawn and quartered at Tyburn, London,
1 July 1616
Beatified by Pope Pius XI on 15 December 1929

NIQUELY AMONG THE English martyrs, Blessed Thomas Maxfield not only ended his days in prison but was born in one. His father, William, had been sentenced to death for harbouring a priest, the martyr Blessed Robert Sutton. William remained in prison until 1606 when he was able to buy his release, dying of natural causes four years later. Blessed Thomas's mother was also under arrest for the same crime.

At the age of about eighteen, Thomas travelled to Douai with his elder brother, Simon, in the hope of being ordained a priest. In 1610, like others before him, he was sent home due to poor health but also, it seems, because the college superiors were uncertain as to whether he was suitable to be ordained. However, he was back two years

later having found himself suspected of 'sedition'. This
time he was deemed ready for ordination to the priesthood, being ordained on 29 March 1614 at Arras.

Returning to England in 1615, Blessed Thomas was only
free for three months before he was arrested by the
pursuivants and held in the Gatehouse prison, Westminster. After questioning he was detained for eight months
before midnight 14–15 June 1616 when he attempted to
escape by means of a rope being let down from his cell
window. He was immediately caught as he reached the
ground and returned to prison where he was savagely
beaten and held in a filthy underground cell before being
transferred to Newgate for trial, charged with being a
priest and with twice refusing to take the Oath of Allegiance, though he was clear that he recognised King James
I as 'his true and lawful sovereign.'

The Spanish ambassador, the Duke of Gondomar,
interceded with the king in the hope of having the sentence
commuted, but to no avail. But the ambassador was able
to send his son and his Dominican confessor to Blessed
Thomas's cell to help him prepare for death. During their
time together Blessed Thomas asked that the ambassador
petition King Philip III of Spain to continue supporting
the English College at Douai from where he had been sent
as 'a soldier of Christ unto war.' declaring proudly that the
college had 'afforded to our poor barren Contrye so much
good and happie seed'.

The Spaniards and some English gentlemen brought
an aura of solemnity into the macabre rites of execution.
The night before, the Spanish ambassador's household
held a vigil of prayer in solidarity with the soon to be
martyr in his cell. Even though the authorities had
attempted to keep the date and time of Blessed Thomas's
execution secret, determining that it take place early in

the morning, a very large crowd had gathered to witness it, somebody even managing to have decorated the scaffold with flowers. As the hurdle bearing Blessed Thomas was dragged through the streets the onlookers witnessed the extraordinary sight of a seeming guard of honour accompanying him as the Spaniards and some English nobles rode on their horses, accompanying the priest, who was wearing his long black cassock and biretta, to Tyburn. Once arrived at the gallows there was a tumultuous scene some taunting but the nobles resolutely demanding that Blessed Thomas be allowed to hang until he was dead before being drawn and quartered, as indeed happened. After the butchery was complete, the Spanish ambassador must have bribed the officials to render to him the remains. Thus, Blessed Thomas's relics can be venerated at Downside Abbey and in various churches in Spain. A more surprising relic is held in the Westminster Diocesan Archives—the calyx of a small pink flower enclosed in a letter. The letter states that Blessed Thomas carried the flower to his martyrdom, clinging on to it until he expired.

BLESSED THOMAS TUNSTAL

Born in Whinfell, near Kendal, date of birth unknown
Hanged, drawn and quartered at Norwich on 16 July
1616
Beatified by Pope Pius XI on 15 December 1929

AVING ENTERED THE English College in 1606, Blessed Thomas Tunstal was ordained a priest four years later and then returned to England. Even though he had taken the precaution of entering the college using an alias—Helmes—and returned to England using a different one—Dyer—Tunstal was arrested almost immediately and spent the next five years in prison. He finally managed to break free from Wisbech Castle but in doing so he injured his hand and had to seek medical help which, in doing so, brought him the attention of the authorities and thus he was rearrested and incarcerated in Norwich gaol.

At his trial, a false witness accused Blessed Thomas of reconciling two Protestants to the Catholic Faith and of trying to convert him. But when the two Protestants were called to give witness themselves they declared that they had never abandoned their beliefs and that the defendant had only encouraged them to lead a holier life. The judge then ordered Blessed Thomas to take the Oath of Supremacy. Declining to do this sealed his fate.

On the scaffold the martyr was asked if he were a Jesuit. He answered that he was not but that he had made a vow to become a Benedictine, requesting that after he had been killed that his head would be displayed on St Benet's gate. Asking what the time was and being told that it was eleven o'clock he said, 'Then it is near dinner time. Sweet Jesus, admit me though most unworthy to be a guest this day at thy table in heaven.' He was granted the mercy of being allowed to hang until dead and of his head being displayed where he had desired.

1618

BLESSED WILLIAM SOUTHERNE

Born at Ketton, Aycliffe, Co Durham, in 1579
Hanged, drawn and quartered at Newcastle upon
Tyne on 30 April 1618
Beatified by Pope St John Paul II on 22 November 1987

UCH WAS THE strength of Catholic faith in the Southerne family that Blessed William's father, being in difficulties with the local authorities due to not conforming to the established religion, sent the ten year old Blessed William to the continent for his education, the future martyr ending up at the Jesuit College in Vilnius, Lithuania. After five years he returned due to poor health but, as soon as he was better, he was sent to Douai College in 1596 though he moved between there and the English College at Valladolid before being ordained a priest in Spain, probably in 1604.

For the next fourteen years he was to minister in the north east of England until his betrayal by a former fellow student from Valladolid. At his trial in Newcastle upon Tyne on 20 April 1618 he was sentenced to death, falling to his knees to thank God upon hearing the sentence. Meanwhile in London, the death of Blessed William became a sticking point in the delicate negotiations between the Spanish and English crowns over the possible marriage of the king's eldest son, Prince Charles, and the Spanish Infanta Maria, a promise that Catholic persecution would cease being part of the marriage agreement. King James was put on the back foot by the news of yet another martyrdom in the north of England and he promised the Spanish king that whoever was responsible would be punished. Duly, Lord Sheffield, President of the Council of the North, was relieved of his position and no priest was to be executed for being a priest in England for the following ten years.

1628

SAINT EDMUND ARROWSMITH

Born in Haydock, Lancashire, in 1585
Hanged, drawn and quartered at Lancaster Castle
on 28 August 1628
Beatified by Pope Pius XI on 15 December 1929
Canonized by Pope St Paul VI on 25 October 1970

F STAUNCH CATHOLIC stock, this martyr was baptised Bryan, choosing the name Edmund upon his Confirmation at Douai, where he had been a student since December 1605. Some months later, poor health compelled him to return to England but he was back in Douai on 15 May 1607, being ordained a priest in Arras on 9 December 1612, setting out for the English mission six months later. He left his college as a secular priest but, having completed the Ignatian spiritual exercises, his heart was being drawn to the Society of Jesus.

Once back in Lancashire, St Edmund worked zealously but perhaps without as much discretion as the times required. He was arrested in 1622 and examined by the Bishop of Chester but was released. In July 1623 he began novitiate as a Jesuit, accounts differing as to exactly how or where this period of formation occurred—it certainly involved at least some time in London. He was admitted to the Society of Jesus in 1624 and was to continue working in Lancashire up until his arrest shortly before the summer assizes of 1628 on Brindle Moss. After being condemned to death for being a priest, St Edmund's last Confession was to St John Southworth who was also imprisoned at that time. After execution the saint's head was displayed impaled on the ramparts of Lancaster Castle, the four quarters of his body being hung from various visible parts of the building. Some parts of his remains and belongings were rescued: one of his hands was kept as a relic by the Arrowsmith family until the martyr's beatification when they gave it to the Catholic Church of Ashton-in-Maker-field and Stonyhurst College holds vestments and other items that were used by the saint.

1641

BLESSED WILLIAM WARD

Born in Westmorland circa 1565
Hanged, drawn and quartered at Tyburn, London,
26 July 1641
Beatified by Pope Pius XI on 15 December 1929

ARD SEEMS TO have been the alias for William Webster who entered Douai College at what was considered to have been an advanced age in 1604. His age notwithstanding it was to be four years before he was ordained a priest on 1 June 1608, setting out for England in October of that year. In the end he did not land in England but in Scotland instead, but still he was captured almost immediately. He spent the following three years in prison after which he crossed the border heading into England. He was arrested again and this time sent to Newgate prison. Over the next twenty years he was in and out of prisons in the London area, ministering inside them to the inmates and to those who came to visit.

Blessed William was arrested for the last time in July 1641 at the house of his nephew in Smithfield, London. It is reported that on the morning of his martyrdom a friend brought him a new coat. Seeing it, Blessed William exclaimed, 'You are right to dress me better than usual, since I am going to a more splendid banquet and a more joyful wedding than any at which I have ever been present.' This buoyancy continued to sustain him on the scaffold when someone stated that he was being executed for seducing the people, Blessed William responding, 'Would to God I had converted more! Nay, even all England!'

Saint Ambrose Edward Barlow

Born in Barlow Hall, near Manchester, November 1585
Hanged, drawn and quartered at Lancaster Castle
on 10 September 1641
Beatified by Pope Pius XI on 15 December 1929
Canonized by Pope St Paul VI on 25 October 1970

EDWARD BARLOW, AMBROSE was to be his name as a Benedictine, was born the fourth of fourteen children to Sir Alexander Barlow and his wife, Mary Brereton. The family were reluctant in their conforming to the Established Church, Edward being baptised in the Church of England parish church of Didsbury on 30 November 1585. In converting to Catholicism Edward followed an elder brother, William, also following him by entering Douai in 1607. Three years later Edward was sent to the Royal College of St Alban in Valladolid, returning to Douai in 1615 and entering the Benedictine community of St Gregory the Great (now Downside) where his brother was prior. The following year, having taken the name Ambrose, the future martyr was professed, being ordained a priest in 1617.

For twenty-four years St Ambrose was to work amongst Catholics living around Manchester and Liverpool and from this time there exist many accounts testifying to his holiness. One such records 'his great zeal in the conversion of souls and the exemplary piety of his life and conversation'. Another writer describes him as being 'so mild, witty and cheerful in his conversation that of all men that ever I knew he seemed to me the most likely to represent the spirit of Sir Thomas More.'. During this time St Ambrose lived at the home of Sir Thomas Tyldesley, Morleys Hall, travelling throughout the area from his base, on the whole avoiding notice.

As St Edmund Arrowsmith was in prison awaiting execution in 1628, St Ambrose gave him the Last Rites. Challoner records that after the former's martyrdom, St Edmund appeared to St Ambrose in a dream, telling him, 'I have suffered and now you will be made to suffer. Say little, for they will endeavour to take hold of you by your words.' Indeed, St Ambrose was arrested on four occasions but was released without charge. This changed after Charles I's proclamation of 7 March 1641 that commanded priests to leave the country or otherwise face the penalties for being a traitor. Six weeks after the king was constrained by parliament to sign the decree, on Easter Sunday, the vicar of Leigh marched with four hundred of his congregation to surround Morleys Hall at the time that St Ambrose was celebrating Mass. The armed crowd encircled the house and took the names of the one hundred and fifty Catholics who had been at the Mass. They were allowed to leave but sixty of the vicar's men escorted St Ambrose to a justice of the peace who sent him on to be imprisoned at Lancaster Castle, where he was held for four months before his trial and condemnation on 8 September, the Feast of the Nativity of the

Blessed Virgin Mary. Two days later he was martyred. His cousin, Francis Downes, was able to rescue his skull and took it to his home, Wardley Hall, where it is venerated to this day. One of the martyr's hands is likewise venerated at Stanbrook Abbey.

1642

SAINT ALBAN ROE

Born in Suffolk in 1583
Hanged, drawn and quartered at Tyburn, London,
on 21 January 1642
Beatified by Pope Pius XI on 15 December 1929
Canonized by Pope St Paul VI on 25 October 1970

ARTHOLOMEW ROE, ALBAN was to be his name in religious life, was to become a Catholic through the simple witness of an uneducated prisoner whom he visited in St Albans. Roe had visited him with the intention of convincing him of the errors of his religion but came away from the encounter with his conscience stirred. As Challoner relates,

> Mr. Roe was very uneasy in mind upon the score of religion; nor did this uneasiness cease till by reading and confessing with Catholic Priests he was thoroughly convinced of his errors and determined to embrace the ancient faith. Having found the treasure of God's truth himself, he was very

desirous to impart the same to the souls of his
neighbours.

Having become a Catholic, Roe made his way to Douai,
entering the college but his energetic zeal and argumen-
tative character coupled with an engaging personality were
deemed to be dangerous to the discipline of the house,
particularly with regard to the influence he was felt to have
on others, and so he was expelled on 16 December 1611.
Early in 1613 he joined the Benedictine community of St
Laurence at Dieulouard in Lorraine (the community that
was to become that of Ampleforth Abbey in Yorkshire)
where he received the name 'Alban' and was ordained a
priest in 1615.

After a brief time in the community of St Edmund's in
Paris, St Alban returned to England, managing to work
covertly for the mission for three years. Most of the rest of
his life was to be spent in prison. He was released in 1623
thanks to the influence of the Spanish ambassador but had
to go into exile. He went to St Gregory's, Douai, but he was
soon back in England, free until being arrested in St Alban's
(the cathedral at St Alban's has a statue of the martyr).

Friends managed to have the monk transferred from St
Alban's to the relative freedom of the Fleet prison in
London where, for seventeen years, he was held by night
but was free to be about town during the day, using his
time to win souls for God. His methods were unortho-
dox—such as playing cards in inns, not for money, but for
prayers to be said—but meant that he was able to reach
parts of society that others could not reach. He also spent
time translating tracts on prayer, ready for publication.

All this came to an end in 1641 when St Alban was
translated to Newgate prison where the conditions were
considerably harsher. In January 1642 he was tried and
found guilty of being a priest, receiving the death sentence

along with Blessed Thomas Green. Together they were dragged to Tyburn on 31 January 1642, St Alban encouraging his companion to the end, each giving the other absolution before their deaths, St Alban's being a 'death showing joy, contentment, constancy, fortitude and valour': he died as he had lived.

Both martyrs were allowed to die by hanging before the rituals of drawing and quartering were accomplished. Devout onlookers collected relics as soon as they could come within touching distance of the carved-up bodies and St Alban's gaolers took advantage of the demand, selling bits of his clothing, some of these relics being now held at Tyburn and Downside.

BLESSED THOMAS GREEN

Born in Warwickshire or Oxfordshire circa 1562
Hanged, drawn and quartered at Tyburn, London,
on 21 January 1642
Beatified by Pope Pius XI on 15 December 1929

THREE ENGLISH COLLEGES were to form Thomas Green as a priest: Douai, Valladolid and Seville. He was ordained in Seville in 1592 before returning to England to minister. He was arrested in the wake of the Gunpowder Plot of 1605 but was fortunate to have been exiled rather than executed, returning swiftly but surreptitiously to continue caring for souls until being a caught for a second time in 1628. On this occasion he was sentenced to death but was reprieved thanks to Charles I's queen, Henrietta Maria, intervening.

Reprieved but imprisoned, Blessed Thomas made the most of his lot and provided spiritual guidance for those who were incarcerated with him and those who came to visit him. In 1635 he was among a number of priests who were freed after paying a bond, widening once more his field of ministry. This was not to last. As Parliament began to assert itself once again in 1640, Catholics were once more persecuted and priests were especially in peril. In January 1642 King Charles had to flee from London leaving the city in the hands of the Parliamentarians. St Alban Roe and Blessed Thomas were both prepared for a traitors' death, the latter being almost eighty years' old by this time. At Tyburn, Blessed Thomas addressed the crowd for half an hour, thanking the sheriff for his patience as he concluded and, after the two martyrs embraced each other, they recited alternate verses of the *Miserere* until the cart on which they stood was dragged away.

BLESSED JOHN LOCKWOOD

Born in Sowerby, Yorkshire, in 1561
Hanged, drawn and quartered at York on 13 April 1642
Beatified by Pope Pius XI on 15 December 1929

WO BROTHERS COMMENCED studying for the priesthood in November 1579: Blessed John, and his younger brother, Francis Lockwood. Blessed John was eventually sent on to Rome, being enrolled at the English College on 4 October 1595 and ordained at the Lateran on 26 January 1597.

He set out for England on 20 April 1598 and forty-four years of hidden ministry ensued, although Challoner relates that he was imprisoned twice during this time. There are records of him being condemned to death on

18 March 1610 but the sentence was commuted to banishment. Finally arrested at Wood End, near Thirsk, the eighty year old priest was condemned to death, suffering with Blessed Edmund Catherick. The older priest asked to be executed first to encourage his younger companion, saying to him:

> My dear brother in Jesus Christ and fellow-sufferer, take courage. We have almost run our race; shall we faint and be tired when in sight of the prize? Let us run in spirit to our Saviour in the garden and call upon him in his agony and bloody sweat ... O Jesus, [let us] lay down our lives in obedience to Thy holy will, and in defence of Thy holy religion, with constancy and perseverance.

The martyrdom of the two priests, especially that of the aged Blessed John, elicited the revulsion of many in York, possibly also that of King Charles I who was in the city at the time and may have hoped to have had the sentence commuted if it were not for the pressure that he was under from Parliament at the time. After being hanged, drawn and quartered, Blessed John's head was displayed on York's Micklegate Bar. Relics of the two martyrs were gathered after their deaths and found their way, thanks to Mary Ward's congregation, to their convent in Augsburg with part of their bodies being preserved and venerated at Downside.

BLESSED EDMUND CATHERICK

Born in Stanwick, Yorkshire, circa 1605
Hanged, drawn and quartered at York on 13 April
1642
Beatified by Pope Pius XI on 15 December 1929

AVING STUDIED AT Douai College and being
ordained a priest, Blessed Edmund commenced
his seven years of ministry about 1635, working
under the alias of Huddleston (probably his mother's
maiden name). He was arrested at Thornton Watlass in
the North Riding and some of the evidence given against
him at his trial may have come from his uncle. Having
shared a hurdle with Blessed John Lockwood, and been
executed with him, Blessed Edmund's head was displayed
on York's Micklegate Bar.

VENERABLE EDWARD MORGAN

Born in Bettisfield, Flintshire, in 1584
Hanged, drawn and quartered at Tyburn, London,
on 26 April 1642

AVING EMBRACED THE Catholic faith through the
work of a Jesuit priest, Fr John Bennett, Edward
Morgan was prepared for priesthood at Douai, St
Omer and the English Colleges in Rome, Valladolid and
Madrid, also testing a possible vocation as a Jesuit. He was
ordained a priest at Salamanca and set out for Britain in
1621. At least some of his ministry was in Wales as he was
arrested there in April 1629, being imprisoned in Flintshire

for refusing to take the oath of allegiance. A worse sentence was to befall him in 1632 when he was condemned to having his ears nailed to the pillory for having accused some judges of treason. After this he was to remain in the Fleet prison until a few days before his death. At his trial on St George's Day 1642 he was condemned for being a priest alongside another priest, John Francis Quashet, a Scottish Minim who was ultimately to die in prison. In the days before his execution Edward Morgan received many visitors, most of whom were eager to take home with them some part of his clothing as a relic. At Tyburn, after praying, he gave a long speech in which he declared 'I offer my blood for the good of my country, and for the procuring of a better understanding between the King and Parliament'. With the rope around his neck, the martyr's good spirits were too clear for an attending Protestant minister who rebuked him for his humour, Edward Morgan declaring, 'Indeed this is no joking matter with me, but very serious; but why should anyone be offended at my going to heaven cheerfully? For God loves a cheerful giver.'

BLESSED HUGH GREEN

Born in London circa 1585
Hanged, drawn and quartered in Dorchester on 19
August 1642
Beatified by Pope Pius XI on 15 December 1929

GOLDSMITH'S SON, BLESSED Hugh left the parish of St Giles-in-the-Fields to be educated at Peterhouse, Cambridge, where he graduated in 1606, being awarded his MA three years later, the same year that he arrived at Douai College, having become a Catholic. He was admitted to the college in 1610, confirmed the following year and ordained a priest on 14 June 1612, leaving for England on 6 August 1612, having briefly considered life as a Capuchin. Thirty years of pastoral ministry lay ahead of him, the latter years having the protection of being Lady Arundel's chaplain at Chideock Castle in Dorset.

In 1642 Charles I issued a proclamation declaring that all priests had to leave the realm by a given date. Blessed Hugh had not seen the proclamation in time but, despite Lady Arundel pleading for him to not risk the journey, he decided to attempt to leave the country travelling to Lyme in the hope of making his way abroad from there. But a custom-house officer, on hearing that he was a priest, pointed out that the period of amnesty was over and duly arrested him, bringing him before a justice of the peace who committed Blessed Hugh to Dorchester gaol. Five months later, on 17 August, he was sentenced to death for being a priest.

After his martyrdom on a hill outside Dorchester, a lady who attended him on the scaffold, Mrs Elizabeth Willoughby, wrote an account of his death that was subsequently published in Brussels. It records how, whilst in prison, Blessed Hugh had converted two women prisoners who died on the same day as him, just before him. The ladies received absolution from him as they prepared to die, just as Blessed Hugh himself received absolution from a Jesuit priest who was present on horseback, disguised as a layman. As he prepared to be martyred, Blessed Hugh gave his handkerchief to the chief gaoler, distributing other belongings to Catholics who were present. He gave a long speech from the scaffold which was occasionally interrupted by Protestant ministers.

Once he had been hung, after seemingly losing consciousness, he was cut down and the disembowelling began. At this point he revived, felt his disclosed bowels with his left hand, making the sign of the cross with his right crying out three times, 'Jesu, Jesu, Jesu, mercy!' Even when the quartering of his body was underway, Blessed Hugh did not expire, causing a woman attending to plead for mercy from the sheriff who promptly ordered that the victim's throat be cut and that he should be beheaded. Blessed Hugh's heart was skewered on a lance and held up for all to see before being thrown into the fire. But the heart rolled away from the fire and was scooped up by Catholic bystander and quickly carried off through the seething crowds. Mrs Willoughby reports how fanatical Puritans danced around the wrecked corpse of the martyr until a sympathetic Protestant lady was allowed to wrap the four quarters of the body in a shroud and bury them near to the scaffold. After the martyr's head was retrieved from the mob who were kicking it around, it too was buried nearby, with sticks thrust into the eyes, ears, nose and mouth.

1643

BLESSED HENRY HEATH

Born at Peterborough, Cambridgeshire, in 1599
Hanged, drawn and quartered at Tyburn, London
Beatified by Pope St John Paul II on 22 November 1987

T WAS AS librarian of Corpus Christi College, Cambridge, that Blessed Henry began to study the writings of the Fathers of the Church and more contemporary works of controversy, becoming convinced of the truth of the Catholic faith. This new knowledge and understanding he could not keep to himself and quickly realizing that his convictions might be dangerous for his life, he abandoned Cambridge and in London was received into the Catholic Church. The Spanish ambassador gave him letters of recommendation for the English College at Douai, where he soon arrived but then moved to the Franciscan convent of St Bonaventure at Douai where he was clothed as a Franciscan in 1623, taking the name of Paul of St Magdalen and, by the end of the year, had been professed.

Blessed Henry remained at his convent for almost nineteen years, being assigned various roles and, in October 1632 he was elected Guardian of the community, a position in which he was reconfirmed in 1634 for three years, being reappointed again in 1640.

Like all the English at Douai, Blessed Henry kept a close watch of the religious and political situation in England, indeed one of his offices whilst at Douai was as *custos custodum*, having a direct care for members of his order in Britain and the Spanish Netherlands. Throughout his ministry he was noted for his personal austerity so it would have come as less of a surprise when he requested to be sent to England in December 1641. To his superiors he wrote, 'You cannot allow that soldier to be a man of courage who, hearing that the army is drawn up in battle array, the drums and trumpets sounding to the charge, and yet shall indulge himself at home in sloth and coward-ice.' Seeking the intercession of English priests condemned to die, he had written to them asking for their prayers: 'Wherefore I humbly beseech you for the love of God, to pray for me that I may come to you and never be separated from you.' In 1643 Blessed Henry's superiors reluctantly agreed to his request.

Walking barefoot the seventy miles to London dis-guised as a sailor, he entered the city begging for lodgings. Being found resting on the steps of a house, the home-owner summoned a constable to remove the man whom he just thought was a vagrant and Blessed Henry was arrested, a document certifying that he was a priest being discovered sewn into his cap. He was not afraid to profess that he was a priest and that he was in England to convert men and women to the Catholic faith and, thus, he was condemned to death. In the year of his death a work that the beatus had written while at St Bonaventure's, *Docu-*

ments of Christian Perfection, was published for the first time, going through six editions and translation into English in 1674. Blessed Henry's saintly life touched many through these writings—his saintly death too, not least his own father, John, who, when widowed and almost eighty years old, went to Douai and was received into the Catholic Church and then the community of St Bonaventure as a lay brother, dying there on 29 December 1652.

1644

BLESSED JOHN DUCKETT

Born in Underwinder, West Riding, in February 1614
Hanged, drawn and quartered at Tyburn, London,
on 7 September 1644
Beatified by Pope Pius XI on 15 December 1929

ORN INTO A landowning Protestant family, Blessed John became a Catholic very young, being admitted to Douai College on 1 March 1633. After ordination to the priesthood in September 1639, he continued his studies in Paris, his life noted for its prayerfulness. Before returning to England he spent two weeks with the Carthusians in Flanders under the spiritual direction of another Fr Duckett, the son of the layman and martyr Blessed James Duckett.

In England, Blessed John ministered in Co. Durham for almost a year until his arrest on 2 July 1644, being caught by soldiers of the parliamentary army at the top of Redgate Banks near Lanchester (a roadside cross marking the place of arrest was erected in 1899). He was caught along with two laymen, on his way to baptize some children. The three were taken to Sunderland where they were examined, Blessed John admitting being a priest in order to save his companions. He was then sent to Newgate prison in London along with the Jesuit priest, Blessed Ralph Corby, who had been arrested near Newcastle. The English Jesuits abroad attempted to arrange exchanging Blessed Ralph for a Scots colonel who was being held a prisoner in Germany. When this appeared to be a real possibility, Blessed Ralph asked his brother priest to take his place in the exchange, feeling that he was better suited to the work of a missionary. Blessed John would not accept, the plan never coming to fruition in any case.

The trial on 4 September was the customary preliminary to the death sentence for both priests but both were permitted to have their heads tonsured and to wear their cassocks for their execution. On the scaffold Blessed John blessed those present, saying little, except to calmly silence a Protestant minister who tried to persuade him to renounce his faith. The two martyrs embraced each other before the cart on which they stood was drawn away, the sheriff present allowing them to die by hanging before the drawing and quartering began. The night before he died, Blessed John wrote to Bishop Richard Smith, Vicar Apostolic of England, who was then in Paris, declaring, 'I fear not death, nor I contemn not life. If life were my lot, I would endure it patiently; but if death, I shall receive it joyfully, for that Christ is my life and death is my gain.'

1645

SAINT HENRY MORSE

Born in Suffolk in 1595
Hanged, drawn and quartered at Tyburn, London,
on 1 February 1645
Beatified by Pope Pius XI on 15 December 1929
Canonized by Pope St Paul VI on 25 October 1970

HE SEVENTH OF nine sons born into the family of Robert Morse, a minor landowner, and his wife Margaret, St Henry was educated at Corpus Christi College, Cambridge, before going on to study law at Barnard's Inn, London. His family were sympathetic to Catholics but conformed to the established religion, St Henry probably becoming a Catholic during his law studies. In 1614, having determined to offer himself for priesthood, he was admitted to the English College, Douai, following an elder brother, William, but had to return to England on family business, being arrested as soon as he landed and imprisoned for four years in the New prison in Clerkenwell, London.

Upon his release from prison in 1618 he returned to Douai before being sent on to the English College, Rome, where he was ordained a deacon in July 1620, seemingly returning to England as a deacon in the same year. There is no record of his priestly ordination, but this had certainly happened by May 1624. Having returned to England St Henry worked for a year and a half in London and then Newcastle before being arrested again in 1626 when attempting to leave the country by sea in order to become a Jesuit. After four years incarceration in York Castle, which he treated as a Jesuit novitiate, he was released and exiled, going to Flanders where he acted as chaplain to English Catholic mercenaries who were enlisted by the Spanish army then engaged in the area.

After some time at the Jesuit house in Liege, St Henry returned to London, working under the alias 'Cuthbert Claxton'. This ministry was particularly dangerous during an outbreak of the plague in 1636 during which he ministered to Catholics and Protestants alike, appealing for funds along with St John Southworth and contracting the disease himself. He recovered from his malaise but, betrayed by a nurse, he was arrested and, in 1637, convicted of being a Catholic priest, being saved from punishment through the intercession of Charles I's wife, Henrietta Maria, and released on grounds of ill health.

Back to work St Henry went, this time in the south-west of England before being arrested yet again on 17 June 1640. On this occasion he was brought before Archbishop Laud but, once again though the powerful influence of the queen, he was released, a decision that was to be used against Laud at his own trial six years later. With the king's declaration of 1641, forced by parliament, St Henry took himself once again to the Netherlands but he could not abandon the Catholics in England for long, returning to his homeland in early 1643, ministering in the north-eastern counties of England. Towards the end of 1644 he was arrested in Cumberland by the parliamentary forces who had just taken Newcastle. Sent to London's Newgate prison, he was sentenced to death on the basis of the conviction of being a priest that he had received eight years earlier, Queen Henrietta Maria having fled abroad and the king being in no position to intervene either.

On the morning of his martyrdom he celebrated a Votive Mass of the Holy Trinity in his cell. Around the scaffold at Tyburn gathered the French, Spanish and Portuguese ambassadors along with their staff, assembled in his honour. As his execution approached, an officer made one last attempt to wring a confession out of the martyr by asking if St Henry knew of any treason against the king or parliament. He answered, 'I have a secret which highly concerns his Majesty and parliament to know.', an astonished and intrigued crowd fell silent. 'Gentlemen, take note. The kingdom of England will never be truly blessed until it returns to the Catholic Faith.'

VENERABLE JOHN GOODMAN

Born in Denbighshire in 1592
Died in Newgate prison in 1645
Declared Venerable by Pope Leo XIII in 1886

HE CONSIDERABLE UNCERTAINTY around the life of this priest is almost certainly the reason why he has not been beatified. A graduate of St John's College, Cambridge (Oxford, says Challoner), ordained an Anglican minister in 1618, the Venerable John Goodman became a Catholic circa 1620 and went to Douai College, seeking ordination. Returning to England as a priest circa 1624 and ministering for some years, he was arrested, tried and sentenced to death but was granted a reprieve by Charles I.

Challoner's account of the Venerable John's life relates that Goodman had been arrested twice before 1642 but had been released until

> [o]nce more a prisoner in 1642, he was brought to trial and condemned to death, but at the queen's intercession was reprieved. When this act of clemency on the part of Charles I excited the anger of Parliament, Goodman, with great magnanimity, protested his unwillingness to be a cause of dissension between Charles and his subjects, and begged that he might be sacrificed to appease the popular displeasure. This heroic act of generosity made a considerable sensation ... Goodman, however, was left to languish in Newgate.

1654

SAINT JOHN SOUTHWORTH

Born in Lancashire circa 1592
Hanged, drawn and quartered at Tyburn, London,
28 June 1654
Beatified by Pope Pius XI on 15 December 1929
Canonized by Pope St Paul VI on 25 October 1970

IN COMMON WITH so many of the Douai martyrs, relatively little is known about St John's ministry in the area of Westminster—the story of the recovery of his relics, the most complete set of relics we have for any of the college's martyrs, can take longer to tell than that of what is known of his life. Yet of all the Douai martyrs, St John Southworth's ministry surely continues to touch the hearts of the thousands of people who see and venerate his shrine in the Chapel of St George and the English Martyrs at Westminster Cathedral and inspire all who see his vested relics in the midst of the prostrate deacons, successors of his as sons of Douai, as they are ordained priests in that great cathedral church.

John Southworth was born into a staunchly Catholic family that had suffered greatly financially for their fidelity to the Faith. In 1613 St John was sent to Douai, receiving the tonsure, then the first step towards ordination, on 24 May 1614. Poor health caused him to return to England in May 1616 but he was able to return to his studies in the spring of the following year and was ordained a priest on Holy Saturday 1618, celebrating his first Mass on Easter Sunday 'with great affection of devotion'.

Southworth spent the following year completing his studies which he concluded by leaving his college to test his vocation as a Benedictine. Which Benedictine house he entered is not known but he did not stay for long as the Douai College diary records that he left the college on 13 December 1619, travelling 'to the vineyard of England.' He remained in the London district until April 1624 when he became a temporary chaplain to the English Benedictine nuns in Brussels.

By 1626 St John was in his native Lancashire where he was soon arrested, imprisoned in Lancaster Castle, tried and condemned to death. Yet he seems to have been reprieved as, in 1628, he was still in Lancaster and able to minister to St Edmund Arrowsmith as he prepared for his martyrdom.

By April 1630 St John was imprisoned in the Clink, an ancient London prison that stood near to the site of Blackfriars Bridge. His name appears on a list of priests who were to be banished but, once again, somehow this did not happen. After the Clink, Southworth was held in the Gatehouse prison, Westminster, where he seems to have been able to bribe the keeper to allow him out to minister secretly to Catholics of the area, a ministry that became particularly critical, and dangerous, during the plague of 1636 when he shared his pastoral care with the Jesuit, St Henry Morse, day after day visiting the homes of the afflicted.

The protecting influence upon Catholics by Queen Henrietta Maria, the wife of Charles I, and the Catholic nobility seems to have played a strong part throughout Southworth's ministry and explains how he was able to survive so many arrests and periods of imprisonment. But Parliament was increasingly aggressive in its Protestant stance and with the civil war, the beheading of the king and the establishment of the Commonwealth, a priest's life was extremely precarious and, in 1654, St John was apprehended at night by a representative of Cromwell.

At his trial the judge urged Southworth to plead 'not guilty' to the charge of being a Catholic priest, but to no avail. The French and the Spanish ambassadors made futile attempts to intervene to save him. On the vigil of the Feast of Saints Peter and Paul, the venerable priest was dragged on a hurdle through the muddy streets to Tyburn where he addressed the thousands present:

> This lesson I have heretofore in my lifetime desired to learn; this lesson I come here to put into practice by dying, being taught it by our Blessed Saviour, both by precept and example. Himself said: 'He that will be My disciple, let him take up his cross and follow Me.' Himself exemplary, practised what he had recommended to others. To follow His holy doctrine and imitate His holy death, I willingly suffer at present; this gallows (looking up) I look on as His cross which I gladly take to follow my dear Saviour. My faith is my crime, the performance of my duty the occasion of my condemnation.

Continuing to speak for longer than the officers charged with the execution could countenance, St John was interrupted and instructed to finish quickly whereupon 'he requested all present who were Catholics to pray for him and with him' and the hangman immediately began his work. St John Southworth was the only priest to be executed under the Protectorate and the last priest to die in England simply for being a priest.

After his body had been beheaded and hacked into four pieces, ready to be displayed at the gates of London, the Spanish ambassador bribed the officers and acquired the body, probably on behalf of the Howard family. After being carefully embalmed the body remained in the Spanish embassy for almost a year until it was taken to the English College, Douai, arriving there on 5 June 1655. There it was venerated until the advance of French revolutionaries caused the college to bury it and other relics for safety. Over time the location was lost and it was only rediscovered by workmen excavating as part of a redevelopment of that area in 1927. Four months after his beatification in 1929, St John Southworth's mortal remains were solemnly enshrined in Westminster Cathedral on 1 May 1930.

1679

BLESSED NICHOLAS POSTGATE

Born at Egdon Bridge, Yorkshire, circa 1597
Hanged, drawn and quartered at York on 7 August
1679
Beatified by Pope St John Paul II on 22 November 1987

HE SON OF prosperous recusant parents, Blessed Nicholas entered the English College at Douai on 4 July 1621, being ordained a priest by the Archbishop of Arras on 20 March 1628. The following year, on the Feast of Sts Peter and Paul, he set out for England where he spent over thirty years as a domestic chaplain in the service, and under the protection, of successive gentry households. This gave him an effective cover for a much wider ministry amongst the Catholics of the areas where he lived and, as this period of his life drew to a close, he was able to write that he had married 226 couples, baptized 593 infants, buried 719 Catholics and reconciled 2,400 to the Catholic Church—and he had 600 penitents to tend to. The letter in which this information is recorded was sent by Blessed Nicholas to Dr George Leyburn,

238 The Douai Martyrs

President of the English College at Douai who, in turn, sent a copy of it to Rome to Cardinal Francesco Barberini, Protector of England. More than numbers, the letter reveals something of the heart of the future martyr:

> I have always worked to help poor Catholics ... I live as a poor man amongst the poor ... I often repeat to myself those words, 'Why look for rest when you were put into the world to labour?' ... what I lack is not the will but help; I am working right to the limits of my strength.

In around 1664 he returned to the North Yorkshire Moors, living in a farmhouse and having a particular care for those living in Egton and Ugthorpe: by 1676 over a third of the adult population in the area was Catholic. The hysteria around the malicious fiction of Titus Oates' 'Popish Plot' brought about Blessed Nicholas's end when, on 7 December 1678, an excise man burst in upon a baptism that the priest was conducting and arrested him. A search of his house ensued wherein was found relics, Catholic books, altar breads and more: plenty of evidence that was used against him at his trial in York in March 1679. Having been convicted, Blessed Nicholas was held at York Castle for four months while the government determined whether or not the policy of executing priests should continue. On 11 July the Privy Council decided that it should and the venerable priest was hanged, drawn and quartered publicly stating that he was dying 'not for the Plot but for my religion'.

Saint John Wall

Born in Lancashire in 1620
Hanged, drawn and quartered at Red Hill, Worcester,
on 22 August 1679
Beatified by Pope Pius XI on 15 December 1929
Canonized by Pope St Paul VI on 25 October 1970

ORN INTO A wealthy recusant Lancashire family, St John Wall was sent to the Douai at the age of thirteen before proceeding to the English College, Rome, when he was twenty-one. In Rome he employed the alias 'John Marsh' and was ordained a priest on 3 December 1645, continuing his studies for a further three years before setting out for England in May 1648. St John spent the next few years working under the protection of recusant Catholic houses until late 1650 when he returned to Douai and entered the Franciscan Convent of St Bonaventure where, on New Year's Day 1651, he was clothed as Brother Joachim of St Anne, his roles in the convent including being novice master.

In 1656 St John returned to England, ministering for the next twenty-two years in Worcestershire, being based for twelve years with the Talbot family at Harvington Hall, near Bromsgrove. By the time of his arrest (December 1678), however, St John had moved to Rushock Court, also near Bromsgrove, and it was there that he was apprehended during a night-time raid, the sheriff's officer having been originally sent there searching for a debtor. St John was imprisoned for five months in Worcester Castle, during which time he reconciled a number of Catholics. After being condemned to death in April 1679, the martyr was taken to London for interrogation by, among others, Titus Oates, who was hoping to be able to implicate the saint in the so called 'Popish Plot'. Oates was unsuccessful and St John was returned to Worcester for the law to take its course. Before martyrdom, he was blessed with the ministrations of a brother Franciscan, Father Leveson, who visited him in prison to hear his Confession, give him Holy Communion and who stood by the scaffold to impart final absolution. The martyr's mangled body was buried in the cemetery at St Oswald's, Worcester, where, for some time after the burial, it was noted that the grass remained green over his grave, by comparison to the mud of the surrounding area.

SAINT JOHN KEMBLE

Born in Rhyd y Car, St Weonards, Herefordshire, in 1599
Hanged, drawn and quartered at Widemarsh
Common, Herefordshire, on 22 August 1679
Beatified by Pope Pius XI on 15 December 1929
Canonized by Pope St Paul VI on 25 October 1970

T JOHN STUDIED for priesthood at St Gregory's College, Seville, from circa 1620, being ordained a priest at Douai on 23 February 1625. For fifty-three years he energetically ministered in Monmouthshire founding mission centres for Catholics. During this time he was mostly based at Pembridge Castle, his brother's home and it was there that he was arrested in November 1678 by Captain Scudamore, whose wife and children were Catholics and ministered to by St John. The saint was dragged through the snow to Hereford gaol, another victim of Titus Oates malicious mendacity. For four months St John was held in prison until he and his friend, the priest and future martyr, St John Lewis, were sent to London for interrogation by the Privy Council. On his return to Hereford gaol St John Lewis was visited by Scudamore's children to whom the saint remarked that their father was the best friend that he had, understood to mean that he had opened the way to martyrdom for him, an outcome that was assured by the summer assizes in which he was condemned to death.

When the undersheriff arrived to bring St John to the place of execution, the saint asked for time to finish his prayers and have one last smoke on his pipe. This being granted, the eighty-year-old priest was then dragged on a hurdle to Widemarsh Common where he was permitted to hang until he was dead, even this taking longer than it should have, before the hangman set to work with his knife. St John's nephew, Captain Richard Kemble, buried his uncle's body in St Mary the Virgin's churchyard, Welsh Newton, though one of the martyr's hands is enshrined in St Francis Xavier Church, Hereford.

1680

BLESSED THOMAS THWING

Born at Heworth Hall, Yorkshire, in 1635
Hanged, drawn and quartered in York on 23 October
1680
Beatified by Pope Pius XI on 15 December 1929

ORN INTO A gentry family, Blessed Thomas Thwing was the nephew of another Douai martyr, Blessed Edward Thwing. He was educated at Douai College and St Omer, being ordained and sent on the English mission in 1665. His first three years of priesthood were spent as chaplain at Carlton Hall, the home of his cousins, the Stapletons. He then opened a school in the family's dower house before, in 1677, becoming chaplain to the Venerable Mary Ward's Institute of the Blessed Virgin Mary at Dolebank, three of his sisters being members of the community and his uncle having given them the house.

It was at Barnbow Hall that Blessed Thomas was arrested during the night of 7 July 1679. Two of his uncle's servants had been dismissed for dishonesty and they wreaked their revenge by reporting a fictitious plot (inspired by the malicious Popish Plot) against the life of the king that was alleged to be fomenting at Barnbow. His uncle, Sir Thomas Gascoigne whose home it was, and his household, including Blessed Thomas, were arrested. It was to be almost a year before Blessed Thomas faced trial and even then the trial was adjourned to the summer assizes. On 29 July he faced the court with one of Sir Thomas's former servants testifying against him claiming that a list of Catholics that was found at Barnbow on the night it was raided was a list of conspirators, whereas it was actually a list of those who were willing to support the new convent. All others arrested were acquitted, but not the priest, who was sentenced separately from others at the assizes simply on grounds of his family's social status. 'I am innocent', Blessed Thomas responded upon hearing his fate, humbly bowing his head and, on 23 October 1680, he became the last Douai priest to be martyred.

INDEX OF NAMES

www.ingramcontent.com/pod-product-compliance
Lightning Source LLC
Chambersburg PA
CBHW031243090426
42742CB00007B/297